ATLAS OF THE AMAZON

PICHONCITO
FLY BOOKS

PICHONCITO
FLY BOOKS

The ideas gathered, interpreted, and presented in this volume are based on the information available during the writing and editing process. Further research may shed new light on or introduce new facts about the topics we address, some of which have been summarized for educational purposes. We don't claim to be exhaustive but rather strive to highlight emblematic and representative species that will pique interest and make it easier to understand the complex natural and social dynamics of the Amazon.

We are grateful to the institutions and specialists committed to understanding and preserving the Amazon. Their work over many years has created a solid body of knowledge that not only allows us to appreciate the region's enormous value but also compels us to commit ourselves to its protection, for the good of all who live on our planet.

Atlas of the Amazon

Editor-in-chief: Adriana Roca
Editor: Karina Villalba
Technical and Ecological Consultant: Lizzy Kanashiro
Research and Composition: Ricardo Guerrero
Illustration and Design: Melissa Siles
Layout: Diana Lizano
Copyediting: María Fe Carranza and Jorge Cornejo
Translation: Emmy Douglas and Laura Healy

Corporate Graphics Commercial
1750 Northway Drive
North Mankato, MN 56003
United States
https://pichoncitoflybooks.com/
R. U. C. 20603234643

June 2026
ISBN: 979-8-218-86005-9

ATLAS OF THE AMAZON

There is a magical place right here on our planet. It is magnificent, vibrant, and teeming with countless forms of life—from tiny insects, colorful birds, silly monkeys, and stealthy cats, to climbing plants, gigantic trees, minuscule mushrooms, and...humans! This place is called Amazonia or the Amazon rainforest.

Geologically formed millions of years ago as a result of a series of fascinating natural phenomena, the Amazon today spans parts of eight South American countries and is home to some of the most complex ecosystems on the planet. It is filled with invisible connections and relationships: every plant, every animal, and every raindrop plays a fundamental role. The people who've lived there for centuries know this well; they treasure ancestral knowledge, and they understand, protect, and pass on the mystery and mystique of the region. There, everything is connected. Nothing happens by chance.

Atlas of the Amazon is an invitation to learn about and celebrate this wonder of nature, to understand how it functions and why it is so important to protect it. Because, although it may seem far away, the Amazon rainforest helps regulate the planet's climate, provides valuable natural resources, and is a habitat for species that exist nowhere else in the world. And it's currently facing very real threats like deforestation, illegal mining, animal trafficking, and climate change.

Pichoncito Fly Books is pleased to present *Atlas of the Amazon*, a project undertaken by scientists and editors, using multidisciplinary research, whose goal is to bring children around the world closer to this impressive region—and its challenges—and to start conversations at home, at school, and in the community, encouraging a personal connection with the rainforest, generating empathy, and sparking wonder.

The Pichoncito team hopes that young readers never lose their sense of wonder at the magnificence of diversity and the mysteries of nature.

Pichoncito Fly Books
Boston, June 2026

Table of Contents

How to Use This Book

What is the Amazon? When was it formed? In which countries is it found? Why is it considered a natural wonder? What are the reasons for its amazing biodiversity? How is it all connected and why should we protect it? In *Atlas of the Amazon*, we want to bring you closer to the biggest tropical forest on the planet—to its ecosystems, its incredible habitat, and its population—so that you can answer these questions and others that may come up while you're reading.

The book is divided into four main sections. The first section is meant to showcase the entire region of the Amazon and all its natural diversity. It also introduces the concepts we'll be using throughout the book, which may be new and, above all, useful. In the second and third sections, we present as many species of Amazonian flora and fauna as possible. We've worked very hard to show the most representative species using detailed illustrations based on scientific information—and sometimes recreated scenes—that will help you imagine how they interact. The fourth and last section focuses on topics related to ecology and conservation so you can become familiar with the threats facing the Amazon.

You can choose to read this book like a journey, from page to page, as if following the course of a river, or you can open up to any section to learn more about an animal, a tree, or a fascinating story about the rainforest. You can also come back here again and again—because the Amazon, like this book, always has something new to reveal.

Below, we'll explain how to interpret the different kinds of information and symbols you'll find throughout the book.

MAIN TEXT
Essential information about the subject presented on each two-page spread.

DEEP DIVES
Additional details to supplement the main text.

WARNING
Indicates that a species is at risk of extinction or is a victim of exploitation.

DANGER
Indicates that a species may pose a risk or cause harm.

STAR
Highlights a notable trait of the species, whether related to its appearance, its population size, or its ecological importance.

FUN FACTS
A close look at an important fact about the topic.

In the pages of this book, you'll find curious and intrepid children—just like you—who are discovering the value of the amazing Amazon. Set off with them!

Welcome to the Jungle!

From the air, the gigantic Amazon rainforest seems endless, like an enormous green blanket stretching out to the horizon, interrupted only by its wide rivers. It appears peaceful and tranquil, but that's only an illusion; in fact, the Amazon rainforest is one of the most active and dynamic regions on the planet, concealing millions of natural treasures, stories, legends, and mysteries. The wondrous animals, which defy the limits of our imagination; the plants of stunning shapes, incredible sizes, and dazzling colors; and the innumerable microorganisms inhabiting every corner form a true system of interconnected life and create some of the most beautiful landscapes on Earth. This region is also home to enigmatic Native communities and a territory where some of the most vibrant cities in the world are flourishing.

Why is it called the Amazon?

According to Greek myth, the Amazons were fearsome female warriors who lived in villages governed only by women. They were so strict about preparing for war that they would cut off one breast to improve their skill with the bow and arrow. In 1542, when Spanish explorers arrived in the South American jungle under the command of Francisco de Orellana, they faced tribes in which they saw women fighting alongside men, and they called the women "Amazons" after the legendary mythical fighters. Over time, this term came to be used as the name of the main river in the area (the Amazon River) and also to refer to the entire region.

And when was it formed?

The Amazon basin has existed for 550 million years, since the Cambrian Period, but the tropical forest appeared long afterward, between 56 and 34 million years ago, according to various theories. Later, changes in the Andes mountain range altered the course of the river and led to the creation of large lakes and swamps.

Finally, about 2.5 million years ago, in the Pleistocene Epoch, the great Amazon River began to flow toward the Atlantic Ocean, creating the immense and vibrant rainforest we know today.

The Amazon is a **drainage basin,** which means it is a territory that includes all the rivers and bodies of water that flow into or are connected to the Amazon River. Fed by all these water sources, the Amazon River acts as the great backbone of the region.

This rainforest covers about **2.6 million** square miles. It spans more than a third of South America and makes up about 5% of planet Earth's surface.

One Rainforest, Many Countries

The Amazon basin covers a large part of South America and extends across eight countries—Brazil, Peru, Colombia, Bolivia, Venezuela, Ecuador Suriname, Guyana—and part of the region of French Guiana.

A Place Teeming with Life

Can you imagine a place where a new kind of living organism is discovered every other day and which is home to 10% of all species on the planet? That's the Amazon—home to 427 mammal species, 1,300 kinds of birds, 370 varieties of reptiles, more than 400 types of amphibians, 3,000 species of fish, and millions of kinds of insects and invertebrates.

But there aren't just animals. It's estimated that there are at least 40,000 plant species in the region, 30,000 of which are endemic, meaning they're found only in this region and nowhere else in the world.

And that's just what we know now—some groups of organisms have barely been studied, and scientists still have a lot to discover. Also, the Amazon territory is so vast and inaccessible that there are still large parts left to explore. For all these reasons, the Amazon rainforest is considered one of the richest sources of life and the most biodiverse region on the planet.

180

new species are discovered every year in the Amazon.

365

types of ants were found in 5 hectares of the Amazon rainforest.

1,000

varieties of fungi can be found in just one gram of soil in the Amazon.

What is Biodiversity?

When we talk about biodiversity, we're referring to the different types of animals, plants, fungi, and microorganisms that can be found in a given area. The greater the variety of species, the greater the biodiversity.

It is like a big puzzle in which each species is a piece with a crucial role in nature's composition and function. For example, bees help plants grow, and trees produce the oxygen that allows us to breathe. They all help each other. By protecting biodiversity today, we help keep our planet full of life, beauty, and health. In this way, animals, plants, and trees will continue to exist and keep providing us with many things we need, like food, medicine, clean air, and much more.

Why Is the Amazon So Biodiverse?

Its biodiversity is due to a combination of factors. First, it is a very old region which, for a long time, remained almost untouched, without much human impact. This allowed organisms to evolve over millions of years without threat and without damage to their natural environment. Second, it is a vast territory containing many kinds of ecosystems. Millions of species proliferate in each one, and they all have unique characteristics that allow them to live in the ecosystem and interact with other organisms that live there. Lastly, the tropical climate (with lots of sun and rain) and the presence of nutrient-rich rivers and lakes are factors that favor biodiversity because they make possible the continuous growth of vegetation and a constant renewal of life.

Who Lives in the Rainforest?

The Amazon region is home to some 44 million people who speak more than 86 languages and about 650 dialects. Its great diversity of languages and cultures is unmatched anywhere in the world.

Its inhabitants have the privilege of living in a place where nature always makes its presence known, but to do so they've had to adapt to demanding conditions, such as extreme heat and intense rain, and learn to coexist with wild animals, which can be very dangerous. Can you imagine if a tarantula, a venomous snake, or a big cat could appear at any moment? In the Amazon, life is intense, and even the mosquitoes never stop biting.

But not all people live the same way. Some are accustomed to modern life, while others remain closely connected to the forest and wildlife. For example, a simple illness like a cold could spell the end for an entire isolated village because these populations haven't developed defenses against many of our common illnesses. That's why any contact with outsiders can lead to contagion and unleash deadly epidemics in these communities.

Indigenous communities are responsible for **domesticating** many of the foods we eat today, like cacao, cassava, chili peppers, peanuts, beans, and numerous fruit trees.

Traditional Amazonian art is typically colorful or features designs that have special significance. It is inspired by nature, by stories of Amazonian culture, or by visions brought on by ayahuasca. Artists use materials from the rainforest—such as seeds, feathers, dyes, and clay—to create fabrics, ceramics, and carvings.

Uncontacted Peoples
These groups don't interact with anyone outside of their clans and stay far away from the rest of civilization. They generally live in inaccessible areas scattered throughout the Amazon rainforest, and they maintain a close relationship with their natural environment. They are also known as "isolated peoples," "peoples in voluntary isolation," or "hidden peoples." It's estimated that there are between 60 and 82 groups with this status today, although the number could be higher because very little is known about them. Since they depend entirely on their natural environment, they are extremely vulnerable to the encroachment of economic activities and the growth of cities in the rainforest. The majority prefer to live in isolation for fear of violence, abuse, and loss of territory, which they have suffered many times.

Indigenous Peoples

These groups have lived in the rainforest for hundreds, or even thousands, of years. They are also known as "Native Communities" or "First Peoples," and there are an estimated 420 such groups throughout the Amazon. Some live in small villages near rivers, while others are spread out in remote places that can only be reached by canoe or on foot. They fish and cultivate small gardens, and they are experts on the plants and animals in their environment. They speak their own languages, preserve much of their ancestral knowledge, and maintain the customs of their ancestors. They can often be distinguished by their traditional clothing. These communities have learned to live in harmony with nature, and, because of their extensive knowledge of the forests, they play a key role in protecting the natural heritage of the Amazon.

Urban Populations

Urban populations live in cities and are made up of people from different backgrounds: both Indigenous people who've migrated from their communities and settlers from other regions and countries. They have schools, hospitals, markets, plazas, and streets. They are in touch with the rest of society and are used to modern technology: cars, motorcycles, appliances, cell phones, and more. Despite living in urban centers, people in some areas face significant challenges, such as a lack of drinking water, electricity, internet, and other basic services.

Milestones in the rainforest's development

- **12,000 years ago:** The first humans arrived in the territory. Little by little, they developed organized societies.
- **16th century:** The Spanish and Portuguese began exploring and made their first contact with Native peoples.
- **17th century:** The first religious missions were established by Europeans who sought to convert the Native people.
- **End of the 19th century:** The rubber boom began, and many settlers moved to the rainforest. Commercial activity intensified, and Amazonian cities grew rapidly.
- **Mid-20th century:** Oil exploration and extraction began in the Amazon. More roads, ports, and other kinds of infrastructure were built.
- **Beginning of the 21st century:** Large-scale natural gas extraction began, primarily with the Camisea Project in Peru.

Some important Amazonian cities

Manaus, Brazil. Located in the heart of the tropical rainforest, it is the main financial center and most important port in the Amazon. It has more than two million residents.

Iquitos, Peru. An important cultural center and dynamic commercial port, it has almost half a million residents.

Belém, Brazil. Found near the mouth of the Amazon River, it is considered the gateway to the Amazon from the Atlantic. It has more than two million residents.

Montane Forests
Located in the far west of the Amazon, where the rainforest meets the Andes Mountains, these forests have extremely rugged terrain. They are the highest-altitude forests in the Amazon, and they are characterized by their vegetation-covered mountains, their waterfalls, and their flora and fauna species, which include butterflies, hummingbirds, orchids, and bromeliads. They are also known as "cloud forests" because they are shrouded in mist, which helps keep the environment very humid.

Lakes or Pools
These calm bodies of water form beautiful natural mirrors. Some are permanent, while others only appear during certain months of the year. Temporary pools form when rainwater collects, and oxbow lakes are created when a river rises, overflows, and, after the flooding subsides, bypasses one of its bends, leaving it isolated. These ecosystems are strategic habitats for birds, fish, reptiles, amphibians, and other animals that go to them to drink or hunt.

Rivers
Rivers are large waterways characterized by their strong currents and mighty flow. They travel thousands of miles like enormous water highways. They don't flow in a straight line but rather have bends and curves; from the sky, they look like huge snakes winding through the rainforest.

They can be classified as blackwater, whitewater (yellowish), or clearwater (transparent), and they are home to millions of aquatic species and a source of life for many others.

Savannah
These large swaths of flat land are covered by grasslands and palm groves. They experience heavy rainfall during certain seasons, but at other times of the year they're very sunny and have dry weather. They are home to fast-running animals that are adapted to flat terrain, like deer and foxes.

One Territory, Many Ecosystems

We often think of the Amazon as one big uniform forest, but it's actually an incredibly diverse region, made up of a wide variety of landscapes and unique spaces. The Amazon is a biome, which means it is a vast region of the planet made up of multiple ecosystems that share key characteristics, like a predominantly warm climate, high humidity, heavy rain throughout much of the year, and a rich biodiversity of flora and fauna. That said, these ecosystems also have notable differences.

Among the most important terrestrial ecosystems in the Amazon are lowland forests, montane forests, and savannahs. There are also predominantly aquatic ecosystems, such as rivers, lakes, and extensive wetlands.

Lowland Forests
These forests cover approximately **85% of the Amazon.** They are located on the great Amazon plain, and they have flat terrain. They are very humid, have abundant vegetation, and are home to some of the tallest trees on the continent.

Wetlands or Swamps
These are areas of flat or low-lying land where water collects, making the soil very muddy. Plants that live here have adapted to the intense humidity and are able to grow in the mud. Wetlands tend to stay flooded throughout the rainy season, and, in the dry season, the numerous pools of water left behind attract many animals. The Pantanal, located in Brazil, is the biggest wetland in the world.

The "Friaje"

The climate in the Amazon is almost always warm, but sometimes it gets very cold. This happens when intense, icy winds blow in from the southern part of the continent and the weather changes for several days. In addition to low temperatures, the sky also becomes unusually cloudy.

Did You Know?

Amazonia is crossed by more than 1,000 rivers, which are the setting for incredible stories and adventures. In addition to providing food, rivers are people's primary mode of transportation. That's why you can see canoes, boats, and even enormous cruise ships moving through their waters. Their ports connect cities and communities and are essential for trade and access to natural resources. In a land as rugged and dynamic as the Amazon, river transport is very efficient.

In Brazil, a long stretch of the **Amazon River** is known as the Solimões River. It is only called the Amazon after it meets the Rio Negro in Manaus.

Because of the rugged terrain, many places in the Amazon **aren't connected by roads.** You can only get to them by river or by air.

The Mighty Amazon

The Amazon River is the longest in the world: it begins in the snowy Mismi Mountain, in Arequipa, Peru, and flows through eight countries before emptying into the Atlantic Ocean in the northeastern Brazilian states of Pará and Amapá. It is also the most voluminous river on the planet, which means it carries the most water. The volume of water is so great that it accounts for one-fifth of all the fresh water that flows into the world's oceans. This river alone carries more water than the world's next three longest rivers combined: the Nile, the Yangtze, and the Mississippi.

It is estimated that the Amazon pours about 230,000 cubic meters of water into the Atlantic Ocean every second. That's the equivalent of 92 Olympic swimming pools! And its force is so strong that even far out at sea, where you can't see the coast, you can still drink fresh water that comes from the river. In some stretches, the Amazon is so wide that you can't see the opposite bank. For all these reasons, it is the basin's most important river and is considered the "backbone" of the entire region.

The “Magic Wave”

The *pororoca*, or tidal bore, is a gigantic wave that forms in the Amazon delta when the river meets the Atlantic Ocean during high tide. It’s as if the ocean launches a massive surge of water against the river’s current, forming a wave that can reach the height of a three-story building and can make as much noise as a thunderclap. Many surfers try to ride this wave because it can travel many miles upriver. It’s an incredible sight!

River without bridges

Did you know that, along the entire length of the Amazon, there are no bridges that cross it? This is not only because the river’s depth and strong currents would make construction difficult but also because the river can change its course and become much wider during the rainy season, making it impossible to calculate a fixed span for bridges.

Great rivers of the Amazon

Amazon	Rio Negro
Marañón	Rio Madeira
Ucayali	Xingu
Caquetá or Japurá	Tocantins

This Is the Rainforest

Imagine the Amazon Rainforest as a big building in which, instead of apartments, there are different plants and animals on each floor. Looking down on it from above, you would see only a roof of green leaves, but if you went inside, you would find that there are many different levels, known as forest strata.

Some animals live at the top, where there is plenty of light and wind, while others prefer the dark, damp corners near the ground. Some species, such as butterflies and monkeys, can move between levels, but others never leave their homes. Thanks to this efficient natural organization, the forest is a place teeming with life where surprises hide around every corner.

The Emergent Layer

The emergent layer is like the top of the skyscraper. Only the tallest trees reach this high—those that can grow to over 150 feet, like the ceiba, the red angelim, the shihuahuaco, and the big-leaf mahogany. Their highest points, or crowns, rise above the rest of the forest and seem to touch the sky. On this level, big monkeys, like howlers and spider monkeys, come out to sunbathe; macaws, parrots, and toucans perch for a rest; and eagles position themselves to scan for their prey from above.

The Canopy

At this level, the branches and leaves of the vast majority of the Amazon's trees come together to form the forest's great "roof." It gets lots of sunlight above and provides plenty of shade below, protecting the lower parts of the forest from the intense heat of the sun. It is home to the vultures and colorful birds of the forest, as well as many monkeys, which find abundant shoots, leaves, and fruits to eat, and sloths, which move slowly through the maze of branches.

The Subcanopy or Middle Layer

On this level, we find medium-sized trees and saplings, all tangled up with climbing plants, palm trees, lianas, and epiphytes. Squirrels and other tree-dwelling animals, especially monkeys, move through this level using branches as pathways and vines as giant ropes to hang from and swing from one place to another.

This level is also home to the fearsome margay, a small climbing cat that spends much of its day in the trees. At this height, you can also see enormous birds, bee colonies, and termite nests attached to tree trunks.

The Understory

The understory is like the forest's first floor, rising from ground level up to about 16 feet high. It's a shady place that gets little sunlight, and it's full of passageways formed by ferns, shrubs, bamboo, and growing branches. This is where the smallest monkeys—like marmosets and lion tamarins—live, where the butterflies flutter, the cocks-of-the-rock fly, and the hummingbirds feed. On this level, spiders spin webs to capture their prey, and ticks wait for animals to pass so they can climb on and suck their blood. This space can be very dangerous because it's within reach of big cats and snakes that coil around branches waiting for their prey.

Trees

Each tree species grows where it is best suited. Some prefer areas with more water, while others prefer areas with more sunlight or shade, or rockier soil. Only a few can thrive in all parts of the Amazon.

The Forest Floor

The big building's dark, damp foundation, this layer is connected to the subsoil and to water sources and is covered with leaves, fallen logs, and enormous roots. Here organic matter (dead animals and plants) decomposes, and everything old is converted to food or fertilizer for new plants, thanks to the work of fungi, insects, worms, bacteria, and other microorganisms. All land animals move through this layer, and you can see long lines of ants, dung beetles, toads, frogs, and creepy-crawly creatures.

Ferocious Hunters

Crouched amid the trees and grass, stealthy and stalking, live the big cats of the Amazon Rainforest. The most agile predators in the jungle, these felids have sharp fangs, pointed claws, keen eyesight, a well-developed sense of smell, and highly sensitive hearing. They are territorial and need large home ranges to survive. Although they can live throughout the Amazon, they prefer territories far from humans to avoid being captured. In these places, they find more food and can hunt undisturbed. Because of their beauty and strength, big cats have fascinated people for millennia. They've been admired and considered sacred beings, and they've inspired many myths and artists.

Jaguar (*Panthera onca*)
Also called the *otorongo*, the jaguar is the king of the Amazon and the most powerful hunter in the region. It is especially good at seeing in the dark, and it has highly developed senses of smell and hearing that allow it to locate animals from far away. Its coat helps it blend in with the vegetation, allowing it to attack its prey by surprise. Its whiskers (or vibrissae) are like antennae that let the jaguar gauge its surroundings. With their help, it can move between branches without touching them or making a sound. In addition, it is an excellent swimmer and tree climber, making it almost impossible to escape from its claws and its terrifying maw. It is between 3 and 6 feet long and weighs between 220 and 330 pounds. It feeds on capybaras, collared and white-lipped peccaries, deer, tapirs, monkeys, caimans, iguanas, and fish.

Black Jaguar

Some jaguars in South America are black, and their rosettes are only visible when seen up close and under sufficient lighting. These are known as "melanistic jaguars."

In 1900, there were more than **100,000 jaguars** on the continent. It is estimated that only 50,000 remain today, most of them in Brazil.

Jaguarundi (*Herpailurus yagouaroundi*)
In shape and color, the jaguarundi looks like an otter or a weasel. It has a rounded head, a long neck, hind legs that are longer than its front legs, and a very long tail. It measures between 19.5 and 31.5 inches long and weighs between 6.5 and 17.5 pounds. It feeds on rodents, birds, and reptiles.

Margay (*Leopardus wiedii*)
Like a monkey, this cat lives in trees, climbing and jumping nimbly from branch to branch. Its hind feet can rotate 180 degrees, so it can climb down tree trunks headfirst while hanging on with its claws, like a squirrel. It measures between 16 and 31.5 inches long and weighs between 4.5 and 11 pounds. It feeds on sloths, monkeys, squirrels, and other tree-dwelling species.

Oncilla (*Leopardus tigrinus*)
The *oncilla*, which is the size of a domestic cat, is the smallest wild cat in South America. It prefers to hunt at night with quick movements. It measures between 15 and 21.5 inches long and weighs between 3 and 7.5 pounds. It feeds on mice, lizards, shrews, birds, insects, and other small prey.

Ocelot (*Leopardus pardalis*)
The ocelot hunts mainly at night and prefers to do so by slowly stalking through the vegetation. It measures between 19.5 inches and 3 feet long and weighs between 15.5 and 35 pounds. It feeds on mice, birds, hares, fish, anteaters, monkeys, and deer.

Puma or Cougar (*Puma concolor*)
A strong, silent hunter, the puma usually catches its prey by the neck and carries it off to a safe place. It is the fourth largest cat in the world and one of the most adaptable mammals—it can live just as easily in the tropical rainforest as it can in the mountains or in colder regions of the continent. It measures between 31 and 45 inches long and weighs between 66 and 242.5 pounds. It feeds on deer, hares, and rodents.

Warning!

We, the big cats of the Amazon, are in great danger because many people hunt us for our fur and fangs. Deforestation and habitat loss also threaten our survival because we have less and less territory where we can mate and search for prey.

Forest Mammals

Big cats aren't the only amazing mammals in the Amazon. All the species on these two pages have found their own ways to live there. Many hunt, eat, sleep, and care for their young high up in the forest. To do so, they've developed special characteristics that keep them comfortable up in the branches and vines: claws to hold on, prehensile tails to hang down, extremely long tongues to reach far, and more. But not everything happens way up high. Fantastic animals live in the understory of the forest, as well. They have specially adapted to life in the tangled-up territory of the Amazon.

Marsh Deer
(*Blastocerus dichotomus*)
The biggest deer in South America, the marsh deer is notable for the impressive antlers that grow from its head. It can measure up to 6.5 feet long and almost 4 feet high and can weigh 330 pounds. It prefers to live in waterlogged environments, like marshes.

Maned Wolf
(*Chrysocyon brachyurus*)
This slender wolf is distinguished by the strip of black hair (mane) that runs along its back. It feeds on small animals and fruit.

White-Lipped Peccary
(*Tayassu pecari*)
This pig-like species is slightly larger than the collared peccary. It gathers in herds of 50 to 300 individuals, which make lots of noise when they're on the move. When something scares them, they take off running in all directions, causing a great commotion in the forest!

In the Amazon basin, **427 species** of mammals have been recorded, which is about 8% of all the mammals in the world.

Giant Anteater
(*Myrmecophaga tridactyla*)
The anteater has an extremely long, sticky tongue that it uses to catch ants, termites, and bees. Its claws are so long that they curl inward, forcing it to walk on the outer edges of its front feet. Including its tail, which looks like a feather duster and is almost as long as its body, the anteater can be 6 feet long—as big as an adult human.

Sloth
(*Bradypus tridactylus*)
What would you call an animal that sleeps almost 18 hours a day and, when it wakes, just lies around in the treetops? A lazy sloth! This animal moves very slowly, hanging on with its three curved claws, and the shape of its jaws makes it look like it's always peacefully smiling. It feeds on berries, fruits, and leaves.

Spectacled Bear
(*Tremarctos ornatus*)
This bear's "spectacles" aren't sunglasses or reading glasses. They're spots around the eyes that distinguish each individual. It is the only bear in South America, and it lives in the cloud forests of the Amazon and in other parts of the Andes.

Coati (*Nasua nasua*)
This animal is related to the raccoon. When it senses danger, it sounds an alarm call and the entire band quickly climbs a tree, then jumps back to the ground and scatters. This surprises their predators so they can escape.

Southern Tamandua or Collared Anteater
(*Tamandua tetradactyla*)
This animal is toothless, but it has a long, sticky tongue that it extends into cracks and insect hiding places. It feeds on ants and termites, but also on bees and honey. It moves through the trees, hanging on with its tail.

Brown-Eared or Western Woolly Possum (*Caluromys lanatus*)
The woolly possum is a marsupial, like a kangaroo or a koala, which means it carries its newborn young in a pouch on its belly where it can nurse them. It uses its long tail to move through the trees.

Giant Armadillo
(*Priodontes maximus*)
This is the biggest armadillo species in the world, and its whole back is covered with plates of armor. It also has strong claws and a long snout that it uses to dig holes and feed on ants and termites, almost always at night.

Tapir or *Sachavaca*
(*Tapirus terrestris*)
The biggest mammal in South America, the tapir can weigh up to 550 pounds. It spends its days sniffing the ground with its small trunk in search of grass and other vegetation, and it likes to stay near lakes and other water sources. Tapir calves have stripes like a zebra's, which camouflage them among the plants so they aren't seen by predators.

Collared Peccary (*Pecari tajacu*)
This porky peccary has a snout like that of a pig, its closest relative. It gives off a strong odor, like chicken soup or stinky cheese, especially when it's scared.

Herbivores

Herbivores play a crucial role in the health of the Amazonian ecosystem because they prevent certain kinds of plants from spreading excessively. At the same time, many also spread seeds, which helps ensure a balanced distribution of plants throughout the region.

Monkeys help **balance** ecosystems by regulating plant life. For example, each day a group of spider monkeys can disperse nearly a million seeds per square mile from over 70 different plant species.

Silly Monkeys!

Sometimes the Amazon is like a big party—trees shimmy, leaves shake, and a chorus of screeches, howls, and roars breaks the calm. It is the rainforest's mischievous monkeys performing their acrobatic leaps, climbing swiftly, and hanging nimbly from vines and branches. These primates spend most of their lives in trees, where they eat, build shelters, and care for their young. The biggest monkeys prefer to be at the very top, the medium ones in the middle, and the smallest in the understory of the forest. More than 100 species of monkeys live in the Amazon region. Some are big and others are so small they can fit in the palm of your hand. Most feed on fruits, seeds, leaves, and herbs, but some also eat very small animals, insects, and eggs.

1. Western Pygmy Marmoset (*Cebuella pygmaea*)
This is the smallest monkey in the world! It measures between 4.5 and 6 inches and weighs around 3.5 ounces, about the size of a tangerine.

2. Howler Monkey (*Alouatta seniculus*)
The male howler's roar is so forceful that it can be heard several miles away. It loves eating young leaves as it basks in the sun.

3. *Titi Monkey* (*Plecturocebus spp.*)
The *titi monkey* is monogamous, meaning it has only one mate in its entire life. When resting, the two mates intertwine their tails. Except for nursing, the male is in charge of caring for the young.

4. Bald Uakari (*Cacajao calvus*)
This monkey has a bald head and a bright red face. It prefers to live in moriche palm trees, where it can eat lots of *aguaje* fruit. It uses its powerful, specialized teeth to crack open the shells of the hardest fruits.

5. Emperor Tamarin (*Saguinus imperator*)
This monkey has long whiskers and strong claws, which it uses to extract food from tree bark. It usually has twins, so it's common to see it carrying two babies on its back.

6. Squirrel Monkey (*Saimiri boliviensis*)
Squirrel monkeys are always on the move! They jump and play in the understory of the forest and can form groups of up to 100 individuals.

7. Spider Monkey (*Ateles chamek*)
The spider monkey has very long arms and legs, and it uses its tail like another arm. As it moves through the treetops, it stretches its limbs and looks like a huge spider.

8. Night Monkey (*Aotus nancymaae*)
This is the only monkey in the Amazon that's active at night. It can hunt insects and escape from predators thanks to its sense of smell and its big eyes, which are adapted for seeing in the dark.

9. White-Faced Saki (*Pithecia pithecia*)
This monkey's forehead and cheeks are covered with white fur.

10. Capuchin Monkey (*Sapajus apella*)
This is the most common monkey on the continent, and it lives practically everywhere in the Amazon. It is very intelligent and knows how to use tools to open its food.

Furry and Curious

Although they are elusive and hard to see, there are lots of rodents in the rainforest. They may not be the flashiest animals in the forest, but they do play a key role in maintaining nature's balance because they help spread seeds and grow new plants. They're also a food source for many predators, such as big cats, snakes, and birds of prey. Their presence is essential to the Amazon's vitality.

1. Capybara
(Hydrochoerus hydrochaeris)
The capybara is so famous that it even has its own catchy song, which went viral. It's the biggest rodent in the world and can weigh up to 145 pounds. Because it lives peacefully alongside other mammals, it is very sociable. It lives near water because it loves to spend its days in pools. Despite its robust body, it is a good swimmer and can stay underwater for up to five minutes. Sometimes it hides underwater for a long time, leaving only its nose and eyes above the surface.

2. Northern Amazon Red Squirrel
(Sciurus igniventris)
This squirrel is a very skilled climber thanks to its claws and its ankles, which can turn all the way around when it climbs down trees. Like any good squirrel, it has very strong teeth and jaws that it uses to crack open hard nuts.

3. Brazilian Porcupine
(Coendou prehensilis)
As charming as it is dangerous, the porcupine is covered in sharp quills. It can't shoot or throw them, but they do stick into animals that try to catch it. It lives in the trees and, with the help of its tail, moves among the branches at night.

4. Pacarana
(Dinomys branickii)
The pacarana is the second largest rodent in South America. It's different from other animals because when nature calls, it doesn't go just anywhere; it uses specific areas as "bathrooms."

5. Lowland or Spotted Paca
(Cuniculus paca)
The paca is nocturnal and feeds on fruit. It is a great reforester because, while it eats, it drops many seeds, which then grow into new trees.

Creatures of the Night

Bats, with their spine-chilling looks and nocturnal habits, have inspired fascinating characters like Dracula and Batman. They are the only mammals that can fly, owing to their wings, which are made up of elastic skin (membrane) stretched between elongated finger bones. Beyond their infamous looks, bats are essential for maintaining nature's balance. Some feed on insects, like mosquitoes; some pollinate flowers, so plants can bear fruit; and some eat fruits, spreading seeds that will grow into new trees and bushes.

1. Greater Bulldog or Fisherman Bat
(*Noctilio leporinus*)
This bat, with its drooping lips and cheeks, looks like a bulldog. It catches shrimp, crabs, and scorpions with its feet and then lifts them to its mouth.

2. Tent-Making Bat
(*Uroderma bilobatum*)
It builds its own roost by making the sides of a large leaf fold down like walls. It sleeps there in a group, squeezed in close to the other bats.

3. Vampire Bat
(*Desmodus rotundus*)
It feeds on the blood of large mammals and birds—including humans! It doesn't suck their blood, like we see in the movies, but rather cuts the skin with its sharp teeth and laps up the blood as it flows out. Its saliva contains anticoagulants, substances that prevent wounds from closing quickly. It is a known carrier of rabies.

4. Flat-Faced Fruit-Eating Bat
(*Artibeus planirostris*)
This is an especially muscular bat that eats fruit and lives in the understory of the forest.

5. Great False Vampire or Spectral Bat
(*Vampyrum spectrum*)
This is the largest bat in all the Americas. Its body can measure up to 6.5 inches, and its wingspan can reach 31.5 inches. It feeds on crickets, frogs, lizards, small birds, and other bats. Although it is carnivorous, it doesn't suck its prey's blood, hence the name "false vampire."

6. Pallas's Long-Tongued Bat
(*Glossophaga soricina*)
This bat loves nectar and pollen. Its tongue can stretch way out, allowing it to reach deep into flowers.

Aquatic Life

Did you know that the rivers of the Amazon are home to ferocious piranhas and *trahira* (a type of predatory fish) that can tear off your finger in just one bite? Or that in these rivers you might find pink dolphins or a fish the size of a small boat? Did you know the rivers are also home to very dangerous eels that could electrocute you just as they do their prey? It's true. Both in the rushing rivers and in the calmer swamps and lakes of the region, you can find some of the most astonishing aquatic species in the world. Life in the forest is amazing, but so is what happens in the water. Otters, manatees, dolphins, and more than 3,000 species of fish interact with frogs, caimans, turtles, and other species in a well-choreographed dance of aquatic life.

Other Amazon Dolphins

Besides the pink dolphin, you can find two other dolphin species in the Amazon: the tucuxi or gray dolphin (Sotalia fluviatilis) and the Bolivian river dolphin (Inia boliviensis), a subspecies of the pink river dolphin that only lives in the Madeira River basin in Bolivia and Brazil.

Amazonian populations use many of these **species for food.** Some communities also use the scales and bones of certain fish in handmade crafts.

1. Pink River Dolphin or Boto (*Inia geoffrensis*)
This dolphin stands out because of its eye-catching color, which becomes more intense as the animal gets older. It's almost blind, but it's still a great swimmer. To navigate, it uses a system similar to that of bats: it emits sounds and processes the echoes using an organ that sticks out of its forehead, called a melon.

2. Giant Otter (*Pteronura brasiliensis*)
The giant otter is the biggest otter in the world. It lives with its family and likes to share food with them. It feeds on fish and, along with the caiman, is the Amazon's main aquatic predator. It is very playful and quick in the water thanks to its flat tail and the shape of its legs and paws. It has a smooth, shiny coat with white spots that make each otter unique, like human fingerprints or jaguars' spots. For decades it has been hunted for its valuable fur, and now it is threatened by the deterioration of its habitat.

3. Amazonian Manatee or Sea Cow (*Trichechus inunguis*)
The Amazonian manatee is a gentle, chubby herbivore with smooth skin. It swims calmly, searching for fruit fallen from trees or aquatic plants to eat. It can grow to nearly 10 feet long and can weigh as much as 1,100 pounds—as much as a cow! It's known as the "river gardener" because, as it eats, it clears the water's surface, allowing light and oxygen to reach the bottom of the rivers. It is one of the most threatened species in the Amazon due to illegal hunting and pollution of its habitat. Many manatees die by getting entangled in fishermen's nets.

4. Red Piranha (*Pygocentrus nattereri*)
The red-bellied piranha has teeth so sharp and jaws so strong that it could tear off your finger in a single bite. It's famous for being a fierce hunter,

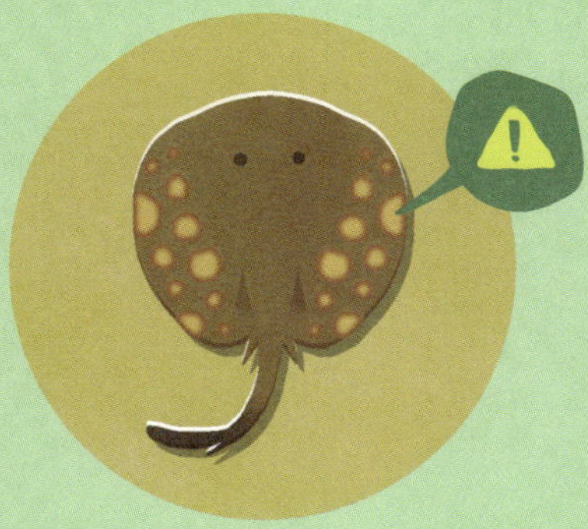

Stingray (*Potamotrygon motoro*)
The stingray has a large stinger at the end of its tail that, when pressed, releases venom that causes very painful wounds. Its body is flat and diamond-shaped, and it doesn't have any scales.

***Payara* or Vampire Fish**
(*Hydrolycus scomberoides*)
The payara gets its nickname from the very large, sharp teeth jutting out of its jaw. When it detects prey, it moves very slowly until it gets close and then quickly attacks.

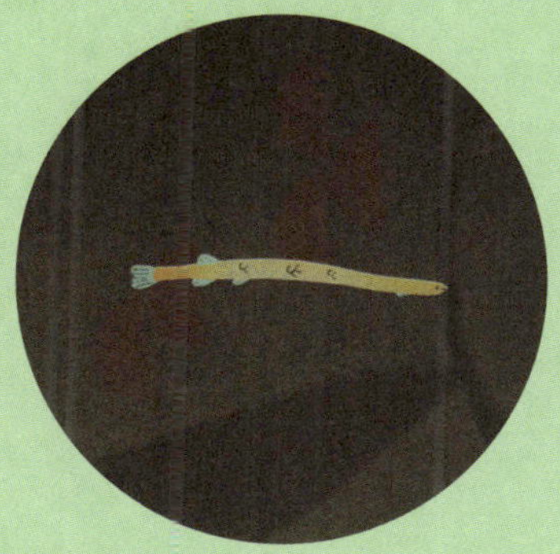

Candiru, Cañero, or Toothpick Fish
(*Vandellia cirrhosa*)
This parasitic fish measures between 0.75 and 1.25 inches. It enters the gills of large fish to suck their blood, like a vampire! Using the spines on its sides, it attaches itself to other fish and feeds off them. It can attack other aquatic animals and even humans.

The scientist John Walsh used eels in his early studies of how electricity works.

but it mainly eats sick or injured fish and dead animals, which gives it an important role in cleaning the ecosystem. It is not the biggest piranha in the Amazon—that title is held by its cousin, the black piranha.

5. Paiche or Pirarucu
(*Arapaima gigas*)
This gigantic fish can grow to almost 10 feet long and can weigh more than 440 pounds. It feeds on smaller fish and can breathe air from the surface of the water thanks to its modified swim bladder, which acts as a lung.

6. Electric Eel
(*Electrophorus electricus*)
This fish can create electricity with its body and use the shocks to hunt prey, defend itself, and even communicate. It can generate more than 600 volts—three times more than the energy we use at home!

7. *Trahira*
(*Hoplias malabaricus*)
This is a voracious fish that can survive for a long time out of water. In swamps or shallow puddles, it can move across damp ground by using its pectoral fins and wriggling its body.

8. Sailfin Catfish
(*Pterygoplichthys pardalis*)
The sailfin catfish has a prehistoric-looking face and a head and body covered with very hard plates. Its whiskers are like antennae that help it find food.

Colorful Feathers

A noisy, colorful flock of birds flying over the Amazon rainforest is a dazzling spectacle. Their trills break the calm, and the flaps of their wings shake the forest. The Amazon is home to more than 1,300 different species of birds, and it is the region with the greatest biodiversity of birds on the planet. Some live only in bamboo forests or swamps, while others range across large territories. In any case, they can be found on all levels of the forest: from the highest treetops down to the ground and everywhere in between.

1. Macaw or Arara (*Ara* spp.)
The Macaw can live up to 40 years and is very sociable, which is why it's usually surrounded by many other macaws. Once it finds a mate, they stay together for life. It feeds on fruit and seeds, but it also eats clay, which contains mineral salts and other substances that protect the macaw from disease and from toxins in its food. That's why it can be seen eating at clay licks with other species of parrots.

2. Yellow-Crowned Parrot (*Amazona ochrocephala*)
This sociable parrot has had a lot of contact with humans throughout history. It's known for its ability to "speak," although it doesn't really talk but rather learns to imitate and repeat the sounds it hears.

3. Hoatzin (*Opisthocomus hoazin*)
This large, prehistoric-looking bird has a prominent crest of feathers and lives on the banks of lakes and rivers. Like the chicken, it doesn't fly much, which is why its chicks have strange claws on their wings to help them climb back into the nest if they fall out. These claws disappear when the chicks reach adulthood. The hoatzin feeds on leaves, and it is the only bird in the world that ferments its food with bacteria in its intestines. This is why it gives off a foul, unpleasant odor, which scares away potential predators.

4. Jabiru (*Jabiru mycteria*)
The Jabiru is a prehistoric-looking stork that can grow to almost 5 feet tall (taller than a ten-year-old child!). It is often seen walking along the banks of large rivers.

5. Jacana or Jesus Bird (*Jacana jacana*)
This bird's long, slender toes allow it to walk on top of aquatic plants, making it look like it's walking on water. That's where it gets the name "Jesus bird."

Beaks of All Shapes

Birds' beaks have evolved to perform different functions, which is why they come in so many different shapes.

Seed-eating: cone-shaped and small, very strong, for breaking seeds.

Curved and Filtering: acts like a sieve to filter food.

Nectar-feeding: long and thin, ideal for reaching nectar in flowers.

Straight: long and sturdy, allows for a varied diet.

Fisher: elongated, for catching fish in shallow water.

Nutcrackers: hooked, designed for peeling fruit and cracking nuts.

All birds play a role in caring for the **ecosystem.** Those that eat fruit spread seeds as they eat, which helps new plants grow. Those that eat insects keep their populations under control and help maintain ecological balance.

6. White-Throated Toucan (*Ramphastos tucanus*)
This toucan has an enormous beak that can grow to be up to a third of its body length. It uses this beak to impress potential mates and intimidate predators.

7. Marvelous Spatuletail (*Loddigesia mirabilis*)
The male of this hummingbird species has a long tail that splits down the middle and ends in two "spatulas" or "rackets" formed by feathers. When it flies, these feathers appear to move on their own, as if they were two small butterflies accompanying the hummingbird. It also has a violet crown and turquoise and blue iridescent feathers on its throat, which glisten in the sunlight.

8. Andean Cock-of-the-Rock or Tunki (*Rupicola peruvianus*)
This bird lives in the Andean cloud forests, in the Amazon's mountainous region. The female is brown, but the male is an intense red or orange color. He has a large crest that goes over his beak, and, when he flies, he looks like a fireball fluttering among the trees. When searching for mates, the males gather to dance, sing, and show off their colors with the goal of attracting females. This performance, known as a "lek," is like nature's talent show.

9. Tropical Royal Flycatcher (*Onychorhynchus coronatus*)
The tropical royal flycatcher has a beautiful, fan-shaped crest that it displays when looking for a mate, when singing, or when it senses a threat. It looks very different when its crest is closed.

10. Amazonian Motmot or Clockmaker (*Momotus momota*)
This bird is called a "clockmaker" because, when it perches on a branch, it moves its long tail back and forth, like the pendulum of a clock.

11. Paradise Tanager (*Tangara chilensis*)
This brilliantly colored bird delights bird watchers in the Amazon basin. It forages in the tree canopy, where it feeds on fruit and insects, and it often gathers in flocks of several different species.

Secret Birds

The Amazon rainforest is home not only to colorful birds whose beauty grabs our attention but also to other less-showy or quieter species whose abilities and characteristics are unique in the animal kingdom. Some are very strong, some are incredibly fast, and others camouflage themselves so well that they can hardly be seen in the dense forest.

Harpy Eagle (*Harpia harpyja*)
This bird's talons are as big as bear claws, and it is so powerful that it can hunt monkeys and sloths in trees. It builds nests high up in the forest, in tree species like the *shihuahuaco,* ceiba, and big-leaf mahogany.

Olive *Oropendola* (*Psarocolius bifasciatus*)
This bird is an expert weaver. It builds hanging nests that look like straw bags and can be almost 6 feet long. It loves to sing and lives in big groups high up in the trees.

Amazon Kingfisher (*Chloroceryle amazona*)
This fast fisherman lives on the banks of lakes and rivers. It sits quietly on a branch and, when it sees a fish, shoots itself into the water like an arrow, catching the fish in its sharp beak.

Kaempfer's Woodpecker (*Celeus obrieni*)
This woodpecker's strong, chisel-like beak allows it to break open tree bark and find hidden insects, which it then catches with its long, sticky tongue. It hits the tree trunks with such force that they echo like drums through the forest.

Razor-Billed Curassow (*Mitu tuberosum*)
This large, elegant bird walks along the forest floor, usually with a partner. Its strong, deep call is like the sound of a far-off drum.

Amazonian Pygmy Owl (*Glaucidium hardyi*)
This small owl is a big nocturnal hunter. It flies silently, and its enormous eyes help it see in the dark so it can hunt insects, lizards, and even little mice. It can turn its head up to 270 degrees, meaning it can turn its head almost completely around and look backward without moving its body!

Osprey (*Pandion haliaetus*)
A superb fish hunter, the osprey dives into the water and, with quick movements, catches its prey with its talons.

Common Potoo, *Kakuy*, or *Urutau* (*Nyctibius griseus*)
When it holds still, this nocturnal bird looks like a tree stump, so it can camouflage itself well and hide from predators. It has a mournful cry that sounds like its Spanish name: "ayaymama..." Its large eyes look even bigger when reflecting the beam of a flashlight in the dark.

King Vulture (*Sarcoramphus papa*)
This large vulture species mainly feeds on carrion and dead animals. Its head has no feathers, making it easier to tear out the innards of its prey. Its sense of smell isn't very good, so it follows other vultures to find food.

Carrion birds are important because they help clean the forest. By eating dead animals, they prevent the carcasses from rotting in the open air and incubating diseases.

Stealthy and Mysterious

These prehistoric animals have lived in the rainforest for millions of years and have adapted to the hot and extremely humid climate. Some, like snakes, can move very quickly, while others, like turtles and caimans, are slower but quite strong. More than 370 reptile species have been recorded in the Amazon, including snakes, lizards, geckos, turtles, and caimans.

Reptiles in the Amazon are **threatened** by hunters who capture them for their skin and meat or to sell them as pets. They are also threatened by deforestation, which destroys their habitat, and by pollution, which contaminates the water and soil where they live.

1. Two-Striped Forest Pit Viper (*Bothrops bilineatus*)
This venomous snake lives in trees and is about 3 feet long. Its color allows it to camouflage itself among the leaves while waiting for its prey. Its venom is powerful and effective.

2. South American Bushmaster (*Lachesis muta*)
Measuring between 6.5 and 13 feet long, this is one of the most dangerous snakes in the Americas. Its venom destroys the tissue of its prey and causes hemorrhages.

3. Green Anaconda (*Eunectes murinus*)
The giant anaconda is the biggest snake in the world. It can grow up to 39 feet long—as long as a bus! Although it is not venomous, it is a good hunter: it catches its prey and squeezes tightly until it stops breathing. It feeds on big animals, like capybaras and small deer, and it can take months to digest its prey.

4. Amazon Broad-Headed Wood Lizard (*Enyalioides laticeps*)
Although it doesn't change color like a chameleon, this lizard's scaly green-and-brown skin helps it camouflage itself in the forest so that it can hunt insects.

5. Yellow-Footed Tortoise (*Chelonoidis denticulata*)
The largest tortoise in South America, the yellow-footed tortoise can grow up to 2.5 feet long. It can live for more than 80 years, and its strong legs allow it to walk long distances in search of food. It eats leaves, fruits, and mushrooms.

6. Amazon Mata Mata (*Chelus fimbriata*)
This turtle has a long neck and an unusual head that makes it look like a leaf. It uses this as camouflage to lure fish into its big mouth.

7. Black Caiman (*Melanosuchus niger*)
The biggest caiman in the Amazon, the black caiman can grow longer than 6.5 feet. At night, its dark skin acts as camouflage in the water.

8. Arrau Turtle (*Podocnemis expansa*)
The biggest freshwater turtle in South America, the arrau turtle can reach more than 2.5 feet in length and weigh over 150 pounds. During breeding season, females travel long distances to lay their eggs on beaches. They can lay more than 100 in a single nest!

9. Yellow-Spotted River Turtle (*Podocnemis unifilis*)
This river turtle spends its days basking in the sun on top of floating logs. It nests on river beaches, but it is at risk because many people hunt it and eat its eggs.

The Forest Choir

The Amazon is home to a diverse collection of frogs and toads whose continuous "croak, croak" chorus can be heard near rivers and ponds, especially at dusk. Amphibians are very special animals because they can live both in water and on land. Unlike reptiles, their skin is usually smooth and moist, although the skin of some species can also be dry and rough. They are often brightly colored to warn predators that they're poisonous.

Right now, we know of more than **1,000 species** of amphibians that live in the Amazon. Of these, 950 are frogs and toads, but there are also salamanders and caecilians, which are legless amphibians similar to worms that live underground or in the mud.

Cane Toad (*Rhinella marina*)
The cane toad is one of the biggest toads in the Amazon. Its skin is brown and rough, and it has poisonous glands behind its eyes that release a toxic substance to fend off predators. It hunts insects, which makes it great for pest control.

Common Suriname Toad (*Pipa pipa*)
This toad lives in water and has a flat, brown body. The most unusual thing about the Suriname toad is that its babies grow on its back. The female carries the eggs in her skin for several weeks until small, fully formed toadlets emerge from her back.

Giant Monkey Frog (*Phyllomedusa bicolor*)
This big green frog lives in trees, and its toes have special discs that help it cling to the branches. Females lay their eggs on big leaves hanging over the water, and, when the tadpoles hatch, they fall right down into the water. Indigenous people of Brazil and Peru use its skin in rituals to prepare for hunting.

Amazonian Bullfrog (Leptodactylus knudseni)
One of the biggest frogs in the region, this bullfrog can grow up to 8 inches, as big as a turtle. Its powerful croak can be heard from far away, and it feeds on small vertebrates, like lizards and other frogs.

Amazon Poison Dart Frog (*Ranitomeya amazonica*)
This is a tiny but mighty, colorful, and very poisonous frog. Indigenous people coat the tips of their hunting darts in its poison. They can make more than 50 lethal arrows with the poison of a single frog! It gets its poison from the insects it eats and uses it to protect itself from predators.

Rococo or Cururu Toad (*Rhinella schneideri*)
This big, round toad has thick skin and lots of warts. When it feels threatened, it can inflate its body to look bigger and scare off predators. Its poison isn't dangerous to humans but can affect some animals that try to eat it.

What's the Difference Between Frogs and Toads?

Frogs jump high, live close to water, and have smooth, moist skin. Toads, on the other hand, prefer to walk rather than jump, can live in drier places, and tend to have rough, dry skin.

Eight-Legged Creatures

In the darkest corners of the jungle, among logs, rocks, and wet leaves, live creepy eight-legged creatures called arachnids. The species that silently stalk this region include giant tarantulas with hairy legs, venomous spiders that can kill a human, and scorpions that patrol the forest with their lethal stingers. Scientists have recorded more than 1,000 varieties of arachnids in the Amazon, but they believe there are still more to be discovered. It's estimated that there could be between 4,000 and 8,000 unknown species!

Despite their terrifying appearance, these arthropods play a fundamental role in nature because they help maintain the balance of the ecosystem. They help control insect populations by eating them, which keeps certain species from becoming too numerous. They are also a food source for other animals, like birds and mammals.

Ogre-Faced Spider (*Deinopis longipes*)
This spider looks terrifying with its big, round, shiny eyes. Instead of weaving a fixed web in which to sit and wait, it shoots out a net to trap its prey, as if it were a fisherman.

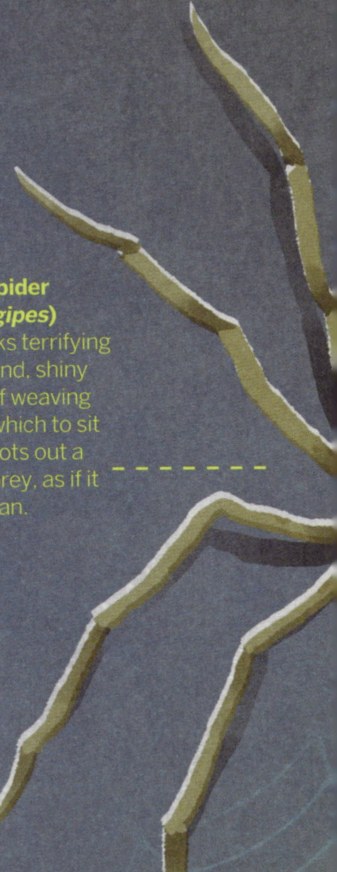

Goliath Birdeater (*Theraphosa blondi*)
This tarantula is the biggest spider in the world. It can have up to a 10-inch leg span—the size of a pizza! It has fangs as long as paperclips, and it's so strong that it hunts not only insects but also frogs, lizards, mice, and small birds. It usually attacks at night.

The venom of the **Goliath tarantula** is not deadly to humans, but it is to small animals.

Social Spiders (*Anelosimus eximius*)
These spiders live in groups of thousands. They care for their young communally and spin their webs together, forming powerful traps to catch insects. Thanks to this teamwork, they can hunt prey that is much bigger than they are.

Brazilian Yellow Scorpion (*Tityus serrulatus*)
This is the most dangerous scorpion in South America, and its venom is powerful enough to kill a human. It can be identified by its bright yellow color.

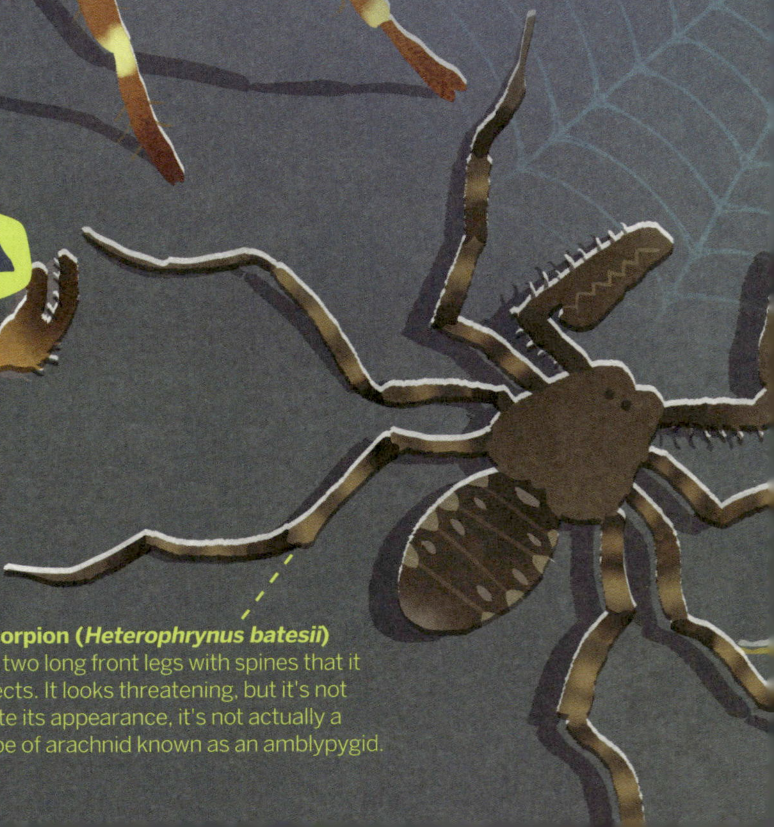

Tailless Whip Scorpion (*Heterophrynus batesii*)
This creature has two long front legs with spines that it uses to catch insects. It looks threatening, but it's not venomous. Despite its appearance, it's not actually a scorpion but a type of arachnid known as an amblypygid.

The banana spider is **fast and aggressive.** It is one of the main causes of arachnid bite injuries in countries such as Brazil.

Brazilian Wandering Spider or Banana Spider (*Phoneutria fera*)
This is one of the most venomous spiders in the world. Its bite causes intense pain, as well as agitation, vomiting, and stomach, lung, and heart problems. It hunts at night and lives in banana groves (where it gets its name). It can have a leg span of nearly 6 inches.

Golden Silk Orb-Weaver (*Trichonephila clavipes*)
This expert weaver spins huge webs between trees, which are used to trap insects and can reach almost 10 feet in diameter. Its silk is the strongest and most resistant in the world. The female is usually found in her web alongside a much smaller spider—the male, who doesn't know how to weave.

Giant Fishing Spider (*Ancylometes* sp.)
This spider runs on top of water to catch its prey. It hunts small fish and frogs in the rainforest's rivers and pools.

Bont Tick (*Amblyomma* sp.)
This parasite is an acarid (a group that includes ticks and mites). It feeds on the blood of animals, such as tapirs, anteaters, and even humans, and it can transmit infectious diseases. After feeding, it can grow to be as big as a grape.

Harvestman or Daddy Longlegs (*Cynorta* sp.)
This arachnid species is characterized by its long, skinny legs and tends to live in large groups. Despite its appearance, it isn't venomous and is completely harmless.

Tiny Inhabitants

Did you know that scientists have found almost a million varieties of insects in the Amazon basin? That's more than any other group in the animal kingdom, and it's estimated that many more species are yet to be discovered! Some insects are great at camouflaging themselves; others can produce deafening sounds or take giant leaps to escape their predators. They can also attack with their powerful venom or glow in the dark. Among the most abundant insects are ants, beetles, termites, butterflies, and bees. But there are so many that it would be impossible to count them, even in a small patch of forest.

Giant Cicada
(*Quesada gigas*)
The male cicada makes a sound so loud that it fills the whole forest, especially at night. It uses this sound to attract females and to gather other cicadas to scare away predators.

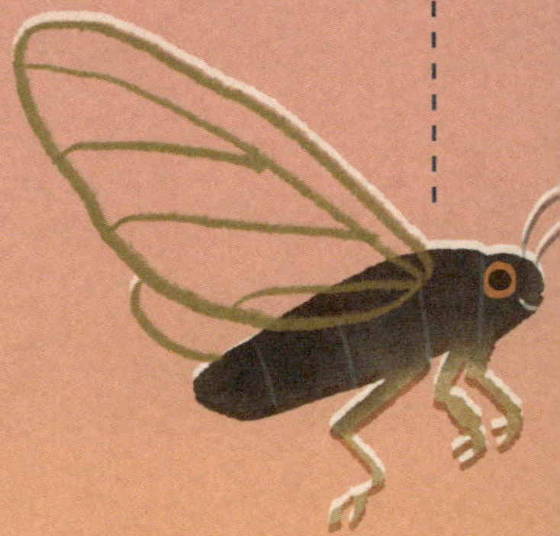

Dung Beetle
(*Coprophanaeus lancifer*)
It collects mammal droppings and rolls them into a ball, which it pushes around and eventually buries. Its work helps fertilize the soil and disperse seeds.

Praying Mantis (*Pseudoxyops perpulchra*)
This mantis gets its name from the way it holds its front legs together in a "prayer" position. These legs are serrated and are used to catch prey, which can even include small birds. It is an expert at camouflage, mimicking a leaf, a flower, or even other insects.

The Amazon is the region with the **greatest number of insects** on the planet. There are estimated to be more than 40,000 species of insects in just one hectare of the Amazon rainforest.

Giant Katydid
(*Stilpnochlora couloniana*)
This katydid can reach almost 3 inches in length and has wings that look like green leaves. Its camouflage allows it to travel through vegetation unseen, but it is a clumsy and inefficient flier. It uses long antennae to sense everything in its surroundings.

Leafcutter Ant (*Atta* sp.)
This ant uses its jaws like scissors: it cuts leaves and carries them back to its anthill. However, it doesn't eat them. It uses the leaves to cultivate a fungus, which is its real food.

Army Ant (*Eciton* sp.)
This carnivorous ant eats other insects, spiders, and small animals. It is very aggressive and moves constantly in enormous groups, attacking any prey that crosses its path, including small animals. Army ants build temporary nests, called "bivouacs," and here's the surprising thing—they don't make them out of leaves or dirt; they build them with their own bodies!

Bullet Ant
(*Paraponera clavata*)
This large ant can grow to over an inch long. The pain of its sting is 30 times more intense than a bee's and lasts up to 24 hours. In some Indigenous groups, such as the Sateré-Mawé of Brazil, young boys must endure its stings to prove their courage during an initiation rite.

Titan Beetle
(*Titanus giganteus*)
One of the biggest beetles in the world, the female titan beetle can reach a length of over 6 inches. Its mandibles are so strong they could easily snap a wooden pencil.

Saber-Toothed Longhorn Beetle
(*Macrodontia cervicornis*)
This very large, very long beetle can grow to almost 7 inches. It stands out because of its huge mandibles and its markings, which look like a harlequin costume.

Stick Grasshopper
(*Apioscelis bulbosa*)
This master of camouflage mimics the shape and color of branches and even moves its body as if it were a branch swaying in the wind. This incredible mimicry protects it from predators. The female is much larger than the male.

Monkey Grasshopper
(*Homeomastax* sp.)
This small grasshopper's brilliant colors—blue, green, red, and yellow—make it stand out against the foliage. It prefers to get around by jumping rather than flying, and it mainly feeds on ferns. Because its antennae are short, its eyes are more developed, helping it better sense its environment.

Insects were the first organisms to develop **wings for flight.** This happened millions of years ago.

Termite
(*Nasutitermes nigriceps*)
Like an ant, the termite lives in colonies and builds large nests that can house millions of individuals. It helps clear plant debris from the forest, recycling its nutrients.

Are Insects Important?

Although they are smaller than other animals, insects play very important roles in the forest. Some work as a team to clean the forest floor, others help recycle plant debris, and others control pests or transport pollen from flower to flower so new plants can grow. Without them, forests simply would not exist.

Owl Butterfly (*Caligo martia*)
This butterfly's back wings have a pattern that mimics an owl's eyes. This feature helps it scare away predators.

Butterfly wings are covered in microscopic scales that reflect light in a special way, giving them their **brilliant colors** and unique patterns. These wings make butterflies the flashiest and most admired insects.

Glasswing Butterfly (*Greta oto*)
This species of "clearwing" butterfly has completely transparent wings.

Juno Silverspot Butterfly (*Dione juno*)
Brilliant orange with black borders, this butterfly is a major pollinator that lives in various Amazonian ecosystems.

Rothschild's Silk Moth (*Rothschildia erycina*)
This nocturnal moth lacks a proboscis, so it cannot reproduce or feed and has a short adult life. Its wings have transparent "windows."

Skeletonized Leafwing Butterfly (*Zaretis itys*)
This butterfly's coloring and shape mimic a dry leaf, which helps it go unnoticed.

Enchanting Wings

A constant vibration envelops the rainforest, like a whisper that never stops: bzzzzzzzzz! Millions of insects are flapping their wings at full speed, day and night, to go searching for food, to reproduce, or to escape predators. These insects play important roles in nature, either as pollinators or as regulators of other organisms' populations. Some produce substances valuable to humans, like honey and silk. This large group of animals includes butterflies, moths, beetles, bees, wasps, dragonflies, mosquitoes, flies, and many other types of insects.

Golden Wasp (*Capitojoppa amazonica*)
This is one of the most terrifying insects in the Amazon because of the way it hunts and parasitizes its victims, like caterpillars, spiders, and beetles. It not only sucks their "blood" and eats them from the inside out; it also lays eggs in them. A few days later, the larvae hatch and feed on their host's carcass until they become adult wasps. This astonishing animal was discovered in 2023 in the Allpahuayo-Mishana National Reserve in Peru.

Blue Morpho Butterfly (*Morpho menelaus*)
The morpho's wings have a characteristic iridescent blue color.

Sara Longwing Butterfly (*Heliconius sara*)
This butterfly can live up to six months, much longer than other species, which have a lifespan of only a few weeks. Its secret? It not only feeds on nectar but also consumes pollen, which gives it additional nutrients and helps it live longer.

Green-Banded Urania Moth (*Urania leilus*)
Unlike most moths, this one flies during the day and has an iridescent green color.

Scarlet Peacock Butterfly (*Anartia amathea*)
This butterfly has an eye-catching red-and-black pattern with white spots.

Great Pondhawk (*Erythemis vesiculosa*)
This nimble dragonfly is a brilliant green color.

Stingless Bee (*Tetragonisca angustula*)
Although this bee can't sting, it can bite.

Human Botfly (*Dermatobia hominis*)
This is the only species of fly that can parasitize humans. Its larvae develop underneath the skin of mammals, which can cause painful lesions.

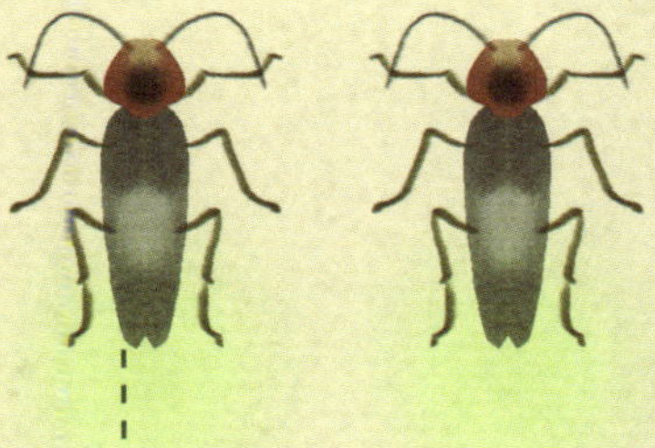

Firefly (*Photinus pyralis*)
When mating, this flying beetle emits flashes of yellowish-green light through a phenomenon called bioluminescence.

The Amazon is home to the greatest diversity of butterflies on the planet. While there are fewer than 500 species in all of Europe, more than

1,300

have been recorded in the Manu National Park in Peru. And new varieties are still being discovered!

Butterfly Kisses

Butterflies love to eat salt. That's why they land on the heads of turtles and drink the tears that fall from their eyes.

Forest Giants

The rainforest is home to imposing trees that can grow to over 260 feet tall and live for more than 700 years. Known as "emergent" trees because they grow taller than the others, they spread their branches out over the top of the jungle like great guardians of the forest.

These giants offer multiple benefits, providing shade during the day, shelter from the rain, and a place to rest. They are home to numerous animals and epiphytes. Their roots contribute to soil stability, and their great size and sturdiness help mitigate strong winds and prevent hurricanes from forming.

Their wood makes these trees valuable, which has unfortunately made them targets of logging and overexploitation, especially in recent years. This situation, along with forest fires and the encroachment of livestock farming into the rainforest, is causing a worrisome decline in the tree population. Their loss not only puts at risk the countless species that depend on them but also poses a serious threat to the entire global ecosystem.

Between 2000 and 2020, the Amazon lost almost **210,000 square miles** of forest. It was estimated that by 2025 that number would have risen to about 300,000 square miles, roughly the size of Turkey.

1. Red Angelim (*Dinizia excelsa*)
This species reaches the highest heights in the Amazon. In the Paru Forest of Brazil, one specimen measures almost 295 feet, as tall as a 30-story building!

2. Ceiba or Kapok Tree (*Ceiba pentandra*)
At the base of this tree's trunk, you can see part of its roots, which look like walls. Inside its fruit, a cotton-like fiber called kapok covers the seeds. This is a dispersal strategy that allows the seeds to be carried by the wind and reach greater distances.

3. Big-Leaf Mahogany (*Swietenia macrophylla*)
Mahogany produces some of the most prized wood in the world, which is why it is one of the most heavily exploited species.

4. Spanish Cedar (*Cedrela odorata*)
Spanish Cedar is a fast-growing species. Its wood is highly sought after, which has led to its classification as Vulnerable.

5. Tornillo (*Cedrelinga cateniformis*)
This tree has very high-quality wood. Its bark yields camphor, which is used for medicinal purposes, and a foam that's used as soap.

6. Sandbox Tree (*Hura crepitans*)
This tree really knows how to defend itself! It has spines on its trunk that protect it from big animals, and its fruit and bark produce toxins that repel insect pests. What's fascinating is that people can use these same substances in agriculture to protect crops, making them an alternative to conventional agrochemicals.

7. Shihuahuaco (*Dipteryx micrantha*)
The shihuahuaco is known as the "steel tree"

because of its very strong, durable wood. Its trunk is so heavy that it can't be transported by river because it sinks the rafts.

8. *Huayruro* or Scarlet Ormosia (*Ormosia coccinea*)
The red-and-black seeds of this tree are used in handmade crafts. They're also believed to have protective powers and bring good luck.

9. Red Ucuuba (*Virola sebifera*)
The fruit of this tree is used to make candles and soaps, and its wood is used to make broomsticks.

Tropical Queens

Though they may look like trees, palms are actually members of a family of primitive plants related to grass, rice, and corn. Nevertheless, in the Amazon ecosystem, they perform many functions similar to those of trees. Among other things, they give shelter to and provide homes for animals, they produce fruit and other foods, and they create shade and regulate environmental temperature.

They're also used in many different ways by humans. The local population uses their stems for building, their broad leaves for roofing, their fruit for food, their oils for cooking and medicinal purposes, their seeds for making artisanal crafts, their spines as arrowheads, and their fibers for weaving and making ropes, mats, hats, bags, toys, and more.

Differences Between a Tree and a Palm tree

Tree	Palm tree
• Its trunk is made of wood. • It has many branches. • Over the years, it grows in height and thickness. • It has bark. • When its trunk is cut, growth rings are visible.	• It does not have wood; it has plant fiber. • It has no branches; it only has large stems and leaves at the top. • Over time, it only grows upward and does not thicken. • It has no bark. • It has no internal rings.

1. Walking Palm (*Socratea exorrhiza*)
This palm can move! It has roots that look like stilts that grow and regenerate throughout its entire life. New roots appear in one direction, while older ones die off and disappear. In this way, the palm tree moves in the direction of its new roots.

2. Açai or Huasaí (*Euterpe precatoria*)
The heart of this palm is known as palmito or chonta, and it is eaten in salads. Its purple fruit is rich in antioxidants and vitamins C and E and is used in desserts and juices. It can grow up to 82 feet tall.

3. Ivory Nut Palm, Tagua, or Vegetable Ivory (*Phytelephas macrocarpa*)
This palm is known as "vegetable ivory" because of its very hard seeds. They are used to make buttons, rings, necklaces, and handcrafted carvings. Its fruit is edible, and its oil is used in cooking. It can grow to over 13 feet tall.

4. Patawa or Ungurahui (*Oenocarpus bataua*)
Patawa fruit is very nutritious; it contains high-quality proteins, comparable to animal protein. This species can grow up to 82 feet tall.

5. Moriche Palm (*Mauritia flexuosa*)
Moriche palm fruit is one of the most distinctive fruits in the rainforest. It's used to make sodas, desserts, and much more. Its sap is used to make drinks and liquors. It can reach a height of almost 115 feet.

6. Chambira (*Astrocaryum chambira*)
Chambira fibers are very strong and are used to make hammocks, backpacks, and fishing nets. It can grow up to 16 feet tall.

7. Mapora Palm (*Oenocarpus mapora*)
Be careful when approaching this palm tree. It's where bullet ants, or isula, prefer to build their nests, and they are very aggressive in defending their territory. This palm can grow to almost 50 feet tall.

8. Sancona Palm (*Syagrus sancona*)
This very adaptable palm tree is so attractive that it's used in many cities to beautify the streets. It can reach over 98 feet tall.

The **oil palm** is used in food, cosmetics, and medicine. It is widely cultivated in the Amazon, and—although it creates jobs and generates income—its cultivation can harm biodiversity and disrupt the region's ecological balance.

Aquatic Plants

In the Amazon rainforest, plants are everywhere, even in the water. Some live deep beneath the surface and others float on top. These plants are homes and shelters for many animals and food for others. Some plants help clean the water by absorbing heavy metals and other pollutants, making them very important to the ecosystem. They grow quickly and can cover large parts of a lake's surface. Sometimes there are so many plants that it becomes hard to travel on the river.

Giant Water Lily (*Victoria amazonica*)
This plant looks like a huge dinner plate floating on shallow water. It can grow to almost 10 feet in diameter and is the biggest floating leaf in the world. It blooms once a year, and only for two days. On the first night, its flower is white when it opens. On the second night, it opens again, but this time its flower is pink. Its veins branch out in a fractal pattern that is not only beautiful but also gives it the strength to support up to 90 pounds (the weight of a child!). For this reason, engineers and architects study it and replicate its design in the structure of many buildings.

Water Lettuce (*Pistia stratiotes*)
Water lettuce is eaten by many animals, such as manatees and capybaras. It has medicinal properties that can help relieve stomach and skin problems.

Water Hyacinth (*Eichhornia crassipes*)
Water hyacinth is distinguished by its beautiful flowers, which appear every two to three weeks. Some toads, frogs, mosquitoes, and fish use its leaves and roots as hiding places. Others lay their eggs in or on the plant.

A Tangled-Up Jungle

If you're exploring the jungle and look upward, you will see that the Amazon, unlike other forests, has an upper layer of trees that's like a vast tapestry of thousands of intertwined plants. This is because the canopy is dominated not only by giant trees but also by a type of plant called climbers. These plants cannot grow on their own, so they use other trees for support as they climb toward the sunlight. Their flexible stems and roots hang from tree trunks and branches or stick to them, as if wrapping them in a hug, and they become bridges that connect the treetops, creating paths for animals to travel and places for them to shelter.

***Huambe* (*Philodendron solimoesense*)**
This philodendron can be recognized by its big heart-shaped leaves. It clings to tree trunks high in the forest, and its long roots grow toward the ground, extending dozens of feet. It produces heat to spread its scent, which attracts insect pollinators.

Strangler Fig or Banyan (*Ficus pertusa*)
This plant is called a strangler because it can wrap around and suffocate other trees, sometimes even killing them. Its seeds lodge into cracks in these trees, and then its roots envelop the whole trunk. When they reach the ground and absorb nutrients, the strangler grows quickly both upward and downward.

Sometimes **climbing plants** are so heavy or so numerous that they can pull down their host trees or cover them completely, suffocating them and depriving them of sunlight, which eventually kills them.

***Tamshi* (*Thoracocarpus bissectus*)**
It germinates on the ground and climbs up trees until it anchors itself to their branches. It then develops long aerial roots, like extremely powerful vines, that descend toward the ground in search of more nutrients for it to continue growing.

Observing the forest, you'll see a wide variety of herbs, shrubs, and other plant species covering the ground like a living carpet or standing majestically throughout the Amazonian landscape. Although these plants don't grow as tall as trees, they play a crucial role in providing shelter and food for different rainforest animals.

False Bird of Paradise (*Heliconia rostrata*)
This eye-catching plant appears to be covered in hanging parrot beaks. In reality, they are colorful bracts (specialized leaves), which cover the interior flowers, making them more attractive to the bats and hummingbirds that come to drink their delicious nectar and carry their pollen to other plants.

Isipó mil hombres (*Aristolochia triangularis*)
This plant catches flies! It attracts them with a strong scent and traps them inside its flower, bathing them in pollen so they can't escape. When the flower dies, the fly is released and flies away, covered in pollen and ready to pollinate other plants.

Climbing plants can be lianas (woody climbers), vines (herbaceous climbers), and philodendrons (climbing plants with large, tough leaves).

Balloon Vine (*Cardiospermum grandiflorum*)
This plant has small flowers and fruit that looks like inflated balloons hanging from its thin, flexible stems. When the fruit dries out and opens, it reveals a black seed with a little white heart-shaped spot. That's why its scientific name means "heart seed."

Colombian Timber Bamboo (*Guadua angustifolia*)
This is a type of bamboo with tall, strong stems that are used to build houses, bridges, furniture, and many other things. Because they are hollow, they can also be used to store drinking water. Bamboo grows easily and can form dense groves. Some species of frogs, birds, and rodents live only in these groves and are known as "bamboo specialists."

Bamboo usually grows in clearings, on riverbanks, and on all kinds of terrain.

Caña brava (*Gynerium sagittatum*)
This type of grass can reach up to 46 feet tall and has stems capped with plumes. When the wind blows, it moves as if it were dancing. This grass is a raw material used in handmade crafts, particularly Colombia's famous *"vueltiao"* hats.

Hot Lips (*Psychotria elata*)
This plant looks like it has bright red, pouty lips, but they're actually bracts, or modified leaves that surround the plant's flowers. They attract animals, such as hummingbirds and butterflies, which come to feed on the flowers, contributing to pollination in the process.

Hanging Gardens

Did you know there's a kind of plant that doesn't grow in the ground but instead grows on other plants? They're called epiphytes, and they live on the trunks and branches of trees, where they extract water from the humid air. This protects them from ground predators and helps them reach the light they need to grow properly. Unlike other species, they don't harm their host plants because they don't take water or nutrients from them; they only use them for support.

There are many varieties of epiphytes. Some, like orchids, are well known, but there are also ferns, bromeliads, and moss. Because of them, the trees of the Amazon appear to be dressed in leaves, flowers, and moss, creating a forest full of shapes, colors, and textures—a magical place.

Orchids

Orchids make up a large family of plants, admired for their strange and beautifully shaped flowers. Many orchids attract insects with their scents, and the insects help them reproduce by transporting their pollen to other plants. Some orchids are small, the size of a coin, and others are famously large, the size of a dinner plate. There are even some that only bloom one day a year. An estimated 18,000 species of orchids exist in the Amazon, 4,000 of them in Colombia.

Ferns

Considered some of the oldest plants on Earth, ferns are distinguished by their lack of flowers and seeds. They reproduce through dust-like spores, which come off the undersides of their leaves. Fern leaves are often long and look like feathers or large green hands that fall from the trees, forming beautiful curtains. Ferns thrive in shady environments with humid air and rain. Some ferns in the Amazon can grow up to 65 feet tall, and they often grow intertwined with one another, forming green layers that drape over trees across huge swaths of the forest.

Bromeliads

Bromeliads are plants with long, hard leaves that grow in a funnel shape that collects rainwater. These small pools of water create a microhabitat for insects, frogs, and tadpoles, and they also provide drinking water for other forest animals. These plants can have beautifully colorful flowers, which attract birds and flying insects, and they help maintain the balance of the ecosystem by providing food and shelter to a wide variety of animals.

Lichens are not simple plants. They are the union of a fungus and an alga that coexist by helping each other out. They are very resistant and grow on trunks, branches, stones, and even leaves. They clean the air and protect trees from the sun and rain.

Mosses

Mosses are tiny, soft plants that form a dense, green carpet over logs, branches, and rocks in forests. Unlike other plants, they lack flowers and deep roots, and they reproduce through spores, like ferns. One of their most notable characteristics is their ability to survive long dry periods, similar to the way bears and other animals hibernate. However, the moment they absorb moisture, they quickly reactivate, and they are essential for storing rainwater for extended periods.

A Gigantic Natural Storehouse

For thousands of years, Native peoples have made the most of the great diversity of edible plants that grow in this region. Over time, they learned to recognize, select, and in some cases domesticate them, and to enjoy their roots, stems, leaves, fruits, and even their sap. Today, these foods form the basis of the local population's diet, and they are valued in many parts of the world.

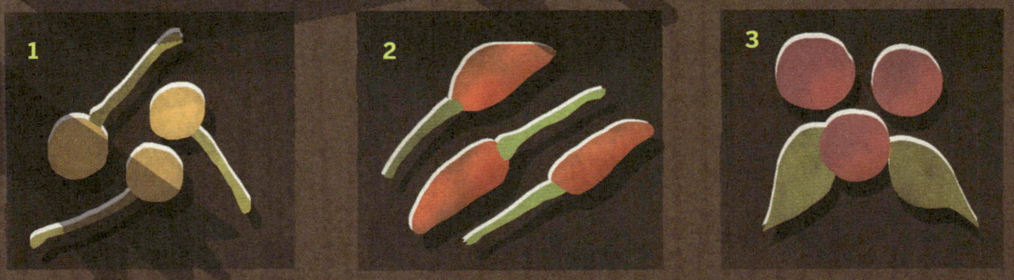

1. *Charapita* Pepper (*Capsicum chinense*)
This is a very potent chili pepper, or hot pepper, that gives many Amazonian dishes their characteristic flavor. It's used in salsas, hot sauces, and dressings.

2. Wild Tabasco Pepper (*Capsicum frutescens*)
This pepper is very spicy and is closely related to the variety used in Tabasco sauce.

3. Camu-Camu (*Myrciaria dubia*)
This is one of the fruits with the highest concentration of vitamin C on the planet. It is mostly consumed in juices and ice creams.

We should **consume** Amazonian fruit **responsibly**. Overharvesting can affect the forest's ecological balance and put all these species at risk. The best way to protect the rainforest for the future is to use its resources without damaging it.

4. Cassava or Manioc (*Manihot esculenta*)
Cassava roots are eaten boiled or fried. They're also used to make an alcoholic beverage called masato.

5. *Mocambo* Tree or White Cacao (*Theobroma bicolor*)
Its pulp is used to make drinks and desserts, and its seeds are roasted over hot coals.

6. Araza (*Eugenia stipitata*)
This fruit is high in vitamins A, B, and C. It is used in juices, jams, ice cream, and even wine.

7. *Cupuaçu* (*Theobroma grandiflorum*)
Cupuaçu is used as a flavoring in ice cream, desserts, liqueurs, and other drinks.

8. Soursop (*Annona muricata*)
This fruit has a sweet pulp that is pulled apart and eaten. It's also used as an ingredient in ice cream and desserts.

9. Guarana (*Paullinia cupana*)
Guarana fruit helps fight illness and is used in energy drinks all over the world.

10. Dragon Fruit (*Selenicereus* sp.)
This fruit has a mild, sweet, and nutritious flavor. It helps the digestive system function properly.

11. Brazil Nut (*Bertholletia excelsa*)
These are big, delicious nuts found inside hard coconut-like fruits called *cocos*.

12. Guava (*Psidium guajava*)
This very nutritious fruit is used in jellies, jams, and soft drinks.

13. Ice Cream Bean (*Inga edulis*)
The pulp of the ice cream bean has a cottony texture and is very sweet. The seeds are a natural laxative.

14. Cacao (*Theobroma cacao*)
This is the wonderful tree that gives us chocolate! It originated in the Amazon but was brought to the north of the continent thousands of years ago. There it was highly prized by civilizations like the Maya and the Aztecs, who consumed it mainly as a bitter drink.

1. Achiote or Annatto (*Bixa orellana*)
Some Amazonian tribes use this plant to paint their bodies, protect their skin from insects and sunburn, and help heal wounds. Its pigments are used in foods and cosmetics.

2. Coca (*Erythroxylum coca*)
Coca grows on the warm slopes of the Andes. Its leaves are natural stimulants and have been consumed as energy boosters since pre-Incan times. This plant can also counteract the symptoms of altitude sickness.

3. Copaiba (*Copaifera officinalis*)
The resin and oil of this plant relieve arthritis pain, reduce inflammation, and help combat infections.

4. Spiked Pepper (*Piper aduncum*)
Spiked pepper has powerful anti-inflammatory and wound-healing properties, and it is used as a pain reliever.

5. Genipap or Jagua (*Genipa americana*)
This plant is used to treat sore throats, digestive problems, and fevers, and it can act as an insect repellent. Its dye is used for skin painting.

6. Ojé (*Ficus insipida*)
The milky white latex secreted from this plant can be used to combat parasites.

7. Dragon's Blood (*Croton lechleri*)
Named for the reddish color of its latex, which has medicinal properties, this plant is used to relieve pain, heal wounds, combat infections, alleviate viral symptoms, and reduce inflammation.

8. Sapucainha (*Carpotroche brasiliensis*)
This plant helps reduce inflammation and treat leprosy.

9. Cat's Claw (*Uncaria tomentosa*)
This climbing plant—whose thorns look like cat claws and help it climb trees—can be used to fight cancer.

10. Quinine or *Cinchona* Bark (*Cinchona officinalis*)
From its bark, we get quinine—a substance used for centuries to treat fever and malaria in many parts of the world. It also flavors tonic water, which is used in cocktails.

11. Ipecac (*Cephaelis ipecacuanha*)
Ipecac is used as an expectorant to alleviate bronchitis and asthma. It also helps treat stomach problems and hemorrhages.

12. *Mashonaste* or *Guariuba* (*Clariciaracemosa*)
The powder obtained from its bark is used to heal wounds and treat skin lesions.

The World Health Organization estimates that 80% of the world's population depends on traditional medicine to meet their basic health needs. Of these, almost **85% use medicinal plants.**

And a Huge Pharmacy!

Did you know the Amazon is home to a huge diversity of medicinal plants with the potential to prevent and cure diseases? Since time immemorial, Indigenous communities have used these plants to strengthen the body and treat various ailments.

Today, these plants are of great interest to the global pharmaceutical industry, and numerous scientists are actively researching their properties to discover new medicines. Given the vast biodiversity of the Amazon, it is believed that its forests may hold the cure for many diseases.

Guardians of the Forest

Something very special lives in the shade of trees and among the damp leaf litter of the rainforest. Neither plant nor animal, they belong to their own biological kingdom: Fungi. When leaves, branches, or trees fall, or when animals die, fungi break down what's left behind and convert it into nutrients for the soil. This provides plants with food so they can grow healthy and strong. Thanks to fungi, the forest stays clean, and the cycle of life is constantly renewed.

Some fungi attract a lot of attention for their bright colors and shapes, which make them look like whimsical sculptures. Others are tiny or grow underground, making them very hard to see. The Native peoples of the Amazon are familiar with many fungi and use them in different ways: to cure illnesses, as food to eat, and to stimulate the mind during rituals. Scientists around the world study them for their medicinal potential and for their role in preserving the environment.

In fiction, the fungus that turns people into zombies in the series *The Walking Dead* and into aggressive creatures in *The Last of Us* belongs to the genus ***Cordyceps***, a family of these Amazonian fungi.

Zombie-Ant Fungus (*Ophiocordyceps unilateralis*)
This fungus can control an ant's brain! First, it invades the ant's body, then feeds on parts of it, and finally takes control of its behavior—forcing the ant to climb to the top of a plant, sink its mandibles into a leaf, and die. The fungus continues to grow until it breaks down the insect's remains, and its spores begin to disperse. By falling from this height, the spores can travel farther and land on other insects.

***Mycena* Mushroom (*Mycena* sp.)**
This mushroom produces its own light through a chemical reaction. It has a very faint glow that can only be seen at night, in the complete absence of light.

Jelly Ear or Wood Ear Mushroom (*Auricularia delicata*)
This is an edible fungus that can be eaten fried, roasted, or boiled. It provides healthy minerals, such as calcium, potassium, magnesium, iron, and zinc, as well as carbohydrates that aid in digestion. It gets its name from its soft, wrinkled surface, which looks like an ear.

Honeycomb Fungus (*Favolus brasiliensis*)
This is a protein-packed edible mushroom with a crispy texture similar to French fries.

Oyster Mushroom (*Pleurotus* spp.)
This edible mushroom is considered a superfood because it contains many essential vitamins and provides protein and antioxidants that help combat illness.

Champagne Glass Mushroom (*Cookeina speciosa*)
This edible mushroom resembles a pink or orange glass.

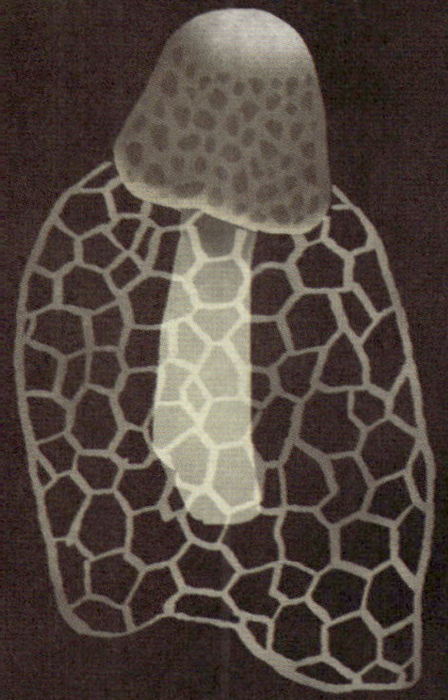

Bridal Veil (*Phallus indusiatus*)
This strong-smelling mushroom appears to be covered with a wedding veil. It can reach a height of almost 10 inches.

Magic Mushroom (*Psilocybe cubensis*)
When eaten, it causes humans to hallucinate. It usually grows on cow dung.

Yanomami Mushroom (*Marasmius yanomami*)
This mushroom is so durable that the native Yanomami people of Brazil use it to make baskets.

Reishi Mushroom (*Ganoderma lucidum*)
This mushroom looks like a big wooden ear sticking out of a tree trunk. It strengthens the human immune system and helps reduce stress and fatigue. Scientists are studying its potential use in cancer prevention.

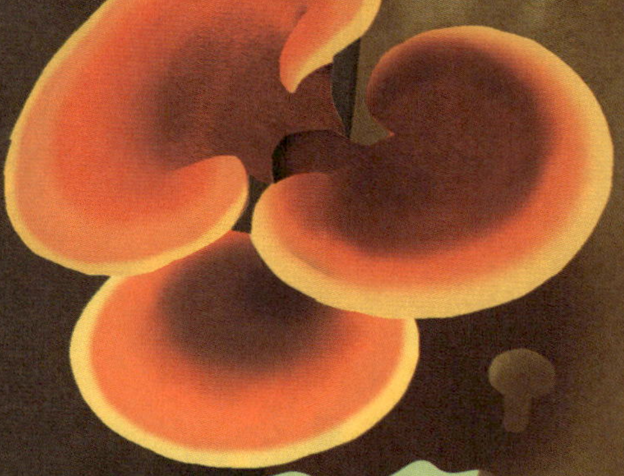

Dead Man's Fingers (*Xylaria polymorpha*)
This mushroom gets its name from its frightening appearance—it looks like a corpse's finger! It helps break down dead wood, but it is toxic to humans.

The Fungus Internet

The scientist Paul Stamets has argued that mycelium, an underground network of fungi, functions as a kind of natural "internet" that connects trees and allows them to share nutrients and send chemical alarm signals. That way, if a tree is attacked by insects or suffers from disease, it can alert nearby trees so they can activate their defenses and survive.

Teamwork?

In nature, many plants and animals depend on other species, and they establish very special relationships with them that can last their entire lives. These relationships are called *symbiosis*, which means "living together."

This form of coexistence is common throughout the world, but in the Amazon—the region with the greatest biodiversity on the planet—we find some surprising interactions. There are three types of symbiotic relationships: mutualism, commensalism, and parasitism.

Mutualism

This type of relationship benefits both species. They work as a team to help each other, protect each other, or simply make each other's lives more pleasant. Everyone wins.

Commensalism

In this type of relationship, only one species benefits, but the other is not affected. It's an alliance in which one species wins, and the other doesn't care and goes along with it despite getting nothing in return.

Parasitism

In this type of relationship, only one species benefits, and the other is negatively affected. It is not a fair relationship, but the adversely affected species can't always avoid it.

Some birds and flying insects feed on nectar from flowers and, in doing so, help the flowers reproduce. When they land on them to feed, their bodies get covered in pollen, which they then transport to other flowers, fertilizing them. In this way, the pollen can reach places the flowers could never get to on their own.

Did you know there are fungi that make trees stronger? They help the trees get nutrients from the soil, while the trees provide them with the sugar they need to grow.

There are also relationships in which one being lives inside another. This is called **endosymbiosis**. An example is when good bacteria live inside our bodies and help us stay healthy.

Did you know there are plants that attach themselves to trees without causing any harm? By doing this, the plants get the nutrients and water they need to grow. They also lend a unique touch to the forest's decor.

Perhaps you didn't know, but there are birds that lay their eggs in other birds' nests, freeing themselves from the responsibility of caring for their own young. The giant cowbird does this; it lays its eggs in the nests of oropendolas so they will feed and take care of their chicks. They are not very responsible parents.

There are also birds that like to eat ticks or fleas off other animals. The birds land on animals to get food, thus removing the animals' annoying pests. While it may not seem like a tasty treat, it is a relationship that benefits both species.

There are bats, like the vampire bat, that feed on the blood of other mammals or birds. Although the bats don't kill them, they do cause wounds and infection and can even transmit diseases. So scary!

Friendly Ant

A special form of symbiosis occurs when some plants become "friends" with ants. The plants offer the ants food and shelter in return for protection. But some ants do more than that: they attack other nearby plants so that only the tree where they live will survive. In this way, they create unique patches in the forest, called "devil's gardens," where only a few species of trees and a single species of ant thrive.

What the Amazon Gives Us

We often overlook the Amazon's countless benefits, which are known as "ecosystem services." They are incredibly varied—from regulating the climate and providing food and natural resources, to offering beautiful landscapes for us to enjoy.

Some of these services are absolutely essential, not only for the communities that live in the region, but also for the entire planet. This place is, without a doubt, a crucial piece in the complex puzzle of life on Earth.

The Amazon

It has: **2.6 million** square miles

Millions of insect species

It has more than: **1,000** species of amphibians

1,000 species of arachnids

And more than: **3,000** species of fish

It is the most biodiverse region on the planet.

It's home to more than: **1,300** species of birds; **427** species of mammals; **370** species of reptiles

The Amazon absorbs 10% of the planet's carbon dioxide. It is the source of 17–20% of all the world's fresh water and **produces 20% of the Earth's oxygen.**

1 It is one of the planet's "lungs" because it gives us clean air. Its forests produce more oxygen than anywhere else in the world and help purify the air.

2 It's like a large air conditioning system that regulates global temperature. It absorbs a lot of carbon dioxide, a gas which, if it accumulates in the atmosphere, can contribute to global warming. Also, because it is a large reservoir of water and moisture, it helps keep the climate cool and balanced throughout the world.

3 It is an important source of fresh water, which keeps millions of humans and animals alive. This water irrigates the land and carries many nutrients to the Atlantic Ocean.

4 It's an enormous source of food, medicine, raw materials, and other natural resources that are very important to the world economy and should be used responsibly and sustainably.

5 It has a wealth of biodiversity. Millions of animal and plant species live and interact there, more than in any other part of the world. Many of these species don't exist anywhere else on Earth. This biodiversity is important because it makes the ecosystem more resilient and allows it to better adapt to climate change, which helps maintain stability around the planet. In addition, biodiversity is like a treasure waiting to be found. Many of the Amazon's species could help us cure diseases and fix problems we don't even know about yet. That's why scientists study them with such intense interest.

6 It's a place filled with opportunities for tourism, recreation, and education.

Threats to the Amazon

Can you imagine if the Amazon's immense riches were lost forever? If its animals went extinct, its plants died, and its rivers and lakes dried up completely? Although it sounds impossible, it could happen in just a few decades if we don't start taking decisive action to protect the environment.

Deforestation

This happens when too many trees in the forest are felled or cut down for various reasons:

- To let grass grow for grazing livestock (mostly cattle)
- To use land for farming
- To get wood from felled trees
- To build large infrastructure projects, like roads, dams, and factories. This doesn't just cause the loss of trees; it also creates easier access to places that used to be more isolated and protected.

The result? Thousands of hectares of forest destroyed or degraded, many wildlife species without homes, and ecosystems more exposed to human activity.

Hunting and Animal Trafficking

This occurs when humans hunt or kill wild animals without respecting the law. Some reasons for this are the following:

- To sell them as pets
- To use their skins, meat, or other body parts
- Simply for fun

The result? Many species are going extinct or are at risk of disappearing. This also disrupts the balance of the ecosystem because each species performs key functions in maintaining the health of the environment.

Imminent Danger: Illegal Activities

Illegal economic activities greatly harm the Amazon rainforest. Because they aren't regulated or controlled, they cause more pollution and deforestation than other activities. They also lack plans and protocols for repairing the damage they may cause to the ecosystem, and they often exploit workers, who have no one to turn to for protection.

One clear example is illegal mining in the rainforest. Many miners, under no supervision, extract minerals with no regard for the environment, polluting rivers and destroying forests. Logging and illicit crop cultivation are the other two major illegal activities increasingly taking place in the Amazon. Their products are extremely valuable on the international market, but getting them causes serious damage to the ecosystem. For all these reasons, it is essential to uphold laws aimed at preserving the forest and demand that the governments of each Amazonian country combat illegal activities.

Pollution

Pollution happens when harmful or toxic substances are introduced to the environment, contaminating the water, soil, or air. It happens, for example, due to gold and mineral mining in the rainforest. This activity uses dangerous chemicals, like mercury, which pollute rivers, harm nearby forests, and affect thousands of plants, animals, and people. It also happens with oil extraction because spills often occur, contaminating everything around them and causing the deaths of many animals. Pollution is also sometimes caused by factories built in the rainforest that don't properly dispose of their waste.

The result? Poisoned rivers and contaminated lakes and forests, which cause illness and death to many living things, altering the natural balance of the forest.

Have you heard of the domino effect? It happens when you line up dominos, push one over, and the others all fall, one after another. Something similar happens in the Amazon: one action leads to others because everything is interconnected. For example, if many trees are cut down, there will be less shade and moisture. This will cause the air to get too warm, and the soil and rivers will dry up more quickly. As a result, animals will lose their homes, they won't find food or water, and they will die. And when this happens, many plants will cease to grow because there will be no one to transport their seeds. So, what starts with the cutting down of trees ends up affecting the entire ecosystem. And if we factor in other threats, like wildfires, contamination, or mining, the future could be devastating.

Earth Is Changing, but Not for the Better

The planet is turning into an oven

Did you know that the planet's temperature is rising more than normal? We are experiencing a phenomenon known as "global warming," which affects ecosystems around the world. This is happening, in part, because there are too many cars and because there are more and more factories emitting greenhouse gases that get trapped in the atmosphere, forming a heat-retaining layer. We're also cutting down lots of trees, so there are fewer and fewer forests to help maintain moisture and regulate temperatures.

The end of the rainforest as we know it

According to scientists, if deforestation reaches 20–25% of the Amazon, its forests could turn into drier ecosystems. This means there would be less rainfall, the soil would be less moist, droughts would be more intense, and many plants and animals that live there would go extinct. This phenomenon is called a "tipping point" because these changes would be irreversible, meaning forever. But this would not only affect the Amazon. If the natural balance of this region is disrupted, the climate of the entire planet would change—for the worse. The Earth would become an increasingly dangerous place, and the lives of all who live here would be at risk.

There's no rain without trees

In many parts of the world, rain is produced when ocean water evaporates and forms clouds. In the Amazon, however, 75% of rainfall depends on water from the forest owing to a natural phenomenon known as "evapotranspiration." Just like humans, plants "sweat," and part of this sweat evaporates in the heat. The same happens when the moist soils of the rainforest heat up and release vapor. All this vapor collects and rises into the sky, forming clouds that bring rain to the Amazon region. But if the forests are destroyed, clouds will no longer form, the water cycle will be interrupted, it will stop raining, and life in the rainforest will be lost.

Humans are **responsible** for climate change, and we are also the only ones capable of reducing or reversing its effects.

The climate has gone crazy

Global warming has caused strange and unexpected changes in the climate. Normally, there are predictable seasons in different parts of the world—cold, warm, rainy, and dry. Now, however, it is hotter than usual in many places, and when the cold arrives, temperatures drop lower than normal. We get more intense rain, floods, and prolonged droughts. All this affects plants, animals, and people, causes disasters, and poses a constant threat to life across the entire planet.

Between 2001 and 2019, 13% of the Amazon was impacted by **large fires**. That's approximately 425,000 square miles, or the size of the entire country of Bolivia.

The forest in flames

In recent years, forest fires have become increasingly dangerous. These large fires burn thousands of hectares of forest, leave millions of species without homes, and pollute the air.

They are often caused by people making campfires or burning fields after a harvest. Other times, they occur naturally due to excessive heat and prolonged droughts caused by climate change.

Both firefighters and the general population work hard to put out the fires, even using helicopters to drop huge amounts of water from the sky. Even so, fires can rage so fiercely that it's almost impossible to extinguish them without the help of rain.

What Can Be Done?

Detection and early warning systems should be improved to respond more quickly to fires, especially during dry spells. We should also take steps to protect the environment and reduce global warming and other effects of climate change.

The Call of the Wild

The Amazon is in danger and needs our help. Its forests are rapidly shrinking and degrading, and many species are at risk of extinction. This situation presents us with one of the most important challenges facing the planet: protecting the delicate balance of nature. But what can we do to protect this natural treasure? A lot!

Heal the Forests

Many parts of the Amazon have already suffered significant damage, so it is crucial to act immediately. For example, we can implement reforestation programs or support natural forest regeneration in degraded areas. Waters contaminated by oil, mercury, and other waste need to be thoroughly cleaned so that these ecosystems can gradually recover and become places teeming with life again. This process, known as "environmental remediation," requires a considerable investment of time and money and the coordinated efforts of governments and various organizations.

Defend Protected Areas

In the Amazon, there are special places called "protected areas," which are large zones where activities that harm the ecosystem are prohibited. Park rangers, or forest rangers, are essential to these places because they are in charge of monitoring, preventing illegal activities, guiding visitors, and collaborating with local communities to promote coexistence with nature. There are also Indigenous territories, home to Native peoples who manage the forest's resources sustainably and defend nature from intruders, thus contributing to the health of forests, wildlife, and rivers. Altogether these protected areas represent almost half of the Amazon region, and they are at risk due to harmful activities.

Support Scientific Research

The Amazon still holds many secrets, so it is vital that we study it. The work of scientists helps us discover new animals and plants, learn how nature works, and understand how to benefit from and protect it. Researching the Amazon isn't easy and requires a lot of work. There are research stations in the middle of the rainforest where scientists can observe, study, and learn. There are also universities and research centers around the world that help process and share information so more and more people recognize the Amazon's importance.

What Can You Do?

You too can be an agent of change in your home and in your community. Each small action helps keep the rainforest alive and well.

1

Consume products from sustainable businesses
You can change your habits and pay more attention to what you buy and consume. Choose products that are certified as having been produced in a sustainable and environmentally friendly way. Doing so will protect nature and help make sure these responsible businesses continue to grow.

2

Avoid keeping wild animals as pets
Keeping wild animals as pets is dangerous for them and for the rainforest. Removing them from their home disrupts their life cycle, stopping entire family groups from reproducing, and many die in the process. Outside their habitat, they don't have the space or food they need to thrive.

3

Get involved and take action!
Join campaigns, petitions, and groups that protect the rainforest. When many people come together, it's easier to ask authorities to protect the forest. You can also share what you know with your family, friends, and teachers. That way, more and more people will care about the rainforest and want to help keep it alive. Learning about the Amazon is one way of protecting it.

4

Support those who protect the rainforest
It's often politicians who permit or encourage the exploitation of the Amazon. That's why it is essential to elect leaders and authorities who are committed to the environment, who pass laws protecting nature, and who take effective measures to conserve forests rather than make decisions that put them at greater risk. If you're not old enough to vote, you can influence those who are.

5

Visit the Amazon
One of the nicest things you can do for the Amazon is to travel there and get to know it better. But remember—always be mindful of the ecosystem and respect local communities. Sustainable tourism is a great way to help. It generates income for those who care for the forest, and, at the same time, allows more people to learn to value the rainforest without harming it.

Glossary

Agrochemical. A chemical used to repel insects and pests from farmland, but which can be harmful to humans and nature.

Amblypygid. A distant relative of spiders. It has long legs and a flattened body and is harmless.

Arboreal. Describes an animal that lives in trees. Monkeys, squirrels, and sloths are examples of arboreal animals, as they spend most of their time climbing around in the branches.

Arthropod. Animals with jointed legs and a body covered by a hard shell, or exoskeleton. Some live on land, others in water, and many have antennae or wings. They include insects, arachnids, crustaceans, and myriapods, among others.

Atmosphere. The layer of air surrounding the Earth, which acts as an invisible shield protecting us from the strong rays of the sun. It also provides us with oxygen to breathe and contributes to the formation of rain and clouds.

Bioluminescence. The process by which some organisms produce their own light.

Bract. A special kind of leaf that protects the flowers of some plants.

Clay lick. A wall or steep bank of mineral-rich clay located along Amazonian rivers.

Course. The path along which river water flows, which can be wide or narrow. It is like a highway along which water travels from one place to another.

Degrade. When something good or healthy, such as a forest, gradually deteriorates and functions less and less effectively.

Decompose. The process by which something that was once alive, such as a leaf or an animal, breaks down into very small pieces until it disappears.

Delta. The point where a river's waters reach the ocean.

Drainage basin. A geographical area where water from rain, snow, springs, evaporation, etc., flows into the same stream or outlet, such as a river or lake. The Amazon is a gigantic drainage basin—the biggest in the world.

Drought. A phenomenon caused by a prolonged absence of rain. The earth dries up, plants wither, and rivers run dry.

Ecosystem. Home to many species, this is a community of living things (animals, plants, and microorganisms) that interact with each other and their environment (soil, water, air, and climate). Each ecosystem has unique characteristics and plays a role in the global ecological balance. For example, an ecosystem can be very important for producing oxygen on the planet, protecting biodiversity, or contributing nutrients to the soil.

Endemic. A species that lives in only one specific place and nowhere else in the world.

Epiphyte. A plant or similar organism that grows on the surface of other plants without harming them, such as moss or lichen.

Fractal. A shape or pattern that repeats over and over, with each small part resembling the larger shape. For example, snowflakes, broccoli, and tree branches.

Germinate. The process by which seeds begin to grow and become plants, sprouting roots and shoots.

Hallucinate. To experience sensations that seem real but are not.

Iridescent. Showing or reflecting rainbow colors, a glint, or a sheen.

Leaf litter. Fallen leaves and other plant debris that accumulate on the forest floor.

Liana. A plant that lacks a strong trunk of its own and so attaches itself to trees to grow and climb. It's a kind of very long, strong vine that grows in the rainforest.

Maw. The back of a ferocious animal's mouth, especially when it is strong, has sharp teeth, and can open wide.

Mitigate. To make something bad or unpleasant less severe, harmful, or serious. For example, if it is very hot, using a fan can mitigate the heat. It doesn't eliminate it completely but makes it more bearable.

Monogamy. When a male and female mate exclusively with each other, a bond which may be temporary or lifelong.

Pollinate. This happens when an animal—such as a bee, hummingbird, or bat—carries pollen from one flower to another. This helps plants produce fruit and seeds so they can reproduce.

Prehensile. Describes something, like a monkey's tail or an elephant's trunk, that can grasp or hold on to things.

Primate. A family of animals that includes monkeys, gorillas, chimpanzees, orangutans, and also humans. They are good climbers and very curious, and some can even use tools or communicate in complex ways.

Proboscis. An elongated, flexible part of the head of some animals—such as an elephant's trunk or a tapir's snout—which helps them feed, grasp things, or simply explore their environment.

Sap. A vital liquid that travels through plants and provides them with all the nutrients they need to grow and live.

Spore. These are like tiny seeds that fungi use to reproduce. They fly through the air or fall to the ground and, if they land in a good spot, grow into new fungi.

Strata. Layers or levels, like the floors of a building, the layers of soil, or the levels of the forest. Different things are found in each stratum.

Toxic. Describes something that can cause harm to people, animals, or the environment if touched, breathed in, or eaten.

Toxin. A substance produced by some animals, plants, or microbes that can harm other living things.

Vibrissae. Long, sensitive hairs that some animals have near their mouth, nose, and even eyes. They help animals detect their surroundings.

Bibliography

1 Burnie, D. (Ed.). (2003). *Earth.* Dorling Kindersley.

2 Ceballos, G., et al. (2010). *Los felinos de América. Cazadores sorprendentes.* Telmex.

3 Emmons, L., & Feer, F. (1999). *Mamíferos de los bosques húmedos de América Tropical: Una guía de campo.* Editorial F. A. N.

4 Gálvez, A., & Aronson, T. (2025). *Plantas del Alto Utcubamba*. Landes, SPDA, Foreslab.

5 Gonzales Coral, A. (2007). *Frutales nativos amazónicos: Patrimonio alimenticio de la humanidad*. Instituto de Investigaciones de la Amazonía Peruana. IIAP.

6 Luhr, J. F. (Ed.). (2005). *Animal: The definitive visual guide*. Dorling Kindersley.

7 Martín-Brañas, M., & Bellido-Collahuacho, J. J. (Eds.). (2022). *Amazonía: Guía ilustrada de flora y fauna*. Ministerio del Ambiente, IIAP, Aecid, APCI.

8 Ministerio de Agricultura del Perú. *Cultivos amazónicos.*

9 OTCA. (2018). *Amazon waters: 10 research projects in the world's largest river basin*. OTCA.

10 Pacheco, V., Inche, B., & Wust, W. (2018). *Mamíferos del Perú*. Grupo La República.

11 Panel Científico por la Amazonía. (2021). *Informe de evaluación de Amazonía 2021.*

12 Programa de Cooperación Hispano-Peruano – Proyecto Araucaria XXI Nauta. (2009). *Amazonía: Guía ilustrada de flora y fauna*. Ministerio del Ambiente, Enlace Regional Loreto, Aecid.

13 Raisg. (2020). *Amazonía bajo presión 2020*. Raisg.

14 Renno, J. F., *et al.* (Eds.). (2005). *Comunicaciones del coloquio internacional: Biología de las poblaciones de peces de la Amazonía y piscicultura*. IIAP, IRD.

15 Salinas, L., Abarca, M., & Wust, W. (2018). *Aves del Perú*. Grupo La República.

16 Schulenberg, T., *et al.* (2010). *Aves del Perú.* Corvidi, Princeton University Press.

17 Silva, S. R., Ximena, L. H. de O., & Martins, M. V. M. (s. f.). *Plantas medicinales del Brasil: Aspectos generales sobre legislación y comercio.* BMZ/Ibama.

18 Stamets, P., & Schwartzberg, L. (2024). *Hongos fantásticos: Para sanar, cambiar consciencias y salvar el planeta.* Editorial Blume.

19 Sumaúma. (s. f.). *La Amazonía de los hongos.*

20 Thorbjarnarson, J. (s. f.). *Black caiman (Melanosuchus niger).* Wildlife Conservation Society.

21 Tratado de Cooperación Amazónica. (1996). *Frutales y hortalizas promisorios de la Amazonía.* TCA, FAO, DGIS, PNUD, ICRAF, FIDA, PNUMA, IICA, GTZ, Unamaz.

22 Vergara, A., *et al.* (2022). *Informe Amazonía Viva 2022*. WWF.

23 Willis, K. J. (2018). *State of the world's Fungi 2018*. Royal Botanic Gardens, Kew.

24 WWF. (2019). *Amazonía Viva! Una década de descubrimientos (2009-2019).*

Articles, Theses, and Pamphlets

1 Ackerman, L., *et al.* (2009). Termite *(Insecta: Isoptera)* species composition in a primary rain forest and agro-forests in Central Amazonia. *Biotropica, 41*(2), 226-233.

2 Barrio-Amorós, C. L., & Manrique, R. (2007). *Observaciones sobre historia natural de la anaconda (Eunectes murinus, Linnaeus, 1758) en los Llanos de Venezuela: Una perspectiva ecoturística*. Fundación AndígenA.

3 Bennett, D. E., Jr., & Christenson, E. A. (1999). *Sobralia altissima. Orchids, 68*(11), 1112–1113.

4 Castro Casal, A., Merchán Fornelino, M., Garcés Restrepo, M. F., Cárdenas Torres, M. A., & Gómez Velasco, F. (2013). Uso histórico y actual de las tortugas charapa (*Podocnemis expansa*) y terecay (*Podocnemis unifilis*) en la Orinoquía y la Amazonia. *Biota Colombiana, 14*(1), 45-64. Instituto de Investigación de Recursos Biológicos "Alexander von Humboldt".

5 Centeno Olarte, J. C. (2023). *Diversidad de helechos arbóreos en un gradiente de elevación – Reserva de Biósfera del Manu* [Tesis de licenciatura, Universidad Nacional de San Antonio Abad del Cusco].

6 Conservación Amazónica – ACEAA. (2024). *Cartilla para capacitación de actores territoriales sobre biodiversidad, cambio climático y NDCs*. Programa Euroclima+, Unión Europea.

7 Cornejo Rodríguez, M. (2024). *Distribución y abundancia de la Paraponera clavata (Hormiga bala) en la localidad de Loma Alta, Provincia de Santa Elena, Ecuador*. Universidad Estatal Península de Santa Elena.

8 Costa, L., *et al.* (2005). Mammal conservation in Brazil. *Conservation Biology*, *19*(3).

9 Cracraft, J. (2022). The hoatzin. *Science Direct*, *32*(20).

10 Cuesta, F., Peralvo, M., Valarezo, N., Hermoza, G., & Moscoso, D. (2009). *Los bosques montanos de los Andes tropicales: Una evaluación regional de su estado de conservación y de su vulnerabilidad a efectos del cambio climático.* Serie Investigación y Sistematización N.° 5. Programa Regional Ecobona – Intercooperation.

11 Dávila, C. (2021). Esfuerzos de conservación del manatí amazónico *Trichechus inunguis* (Natterer, 1833) en el Perú: una revisión actualizada. *The Biologist*, *19*(2).

12 Dourojeanni, M. (2019). Conservación de insectos en la Amazonia. *Ecología Aplicada*, *18*(2).

13 Duplaix, N. (1980). Observations on the ecology and behavior of the giant river otter *Pteronura brasiliensis* in Suriname. *Revue d'Écologie*, *34*.

14 Evans, H. C., Elliot, S. L., & Hughes, D. P. (2011). Hidden diversity behind the zombie-ant fungus *Ophiocordyceps unilateralis*: Four new species described from carpenter ants in Minas Gerais, Brazil. *PLOS One*. https://doi.org/10.1371/journal.pone.0017024

15 Gutiérrez, K., Morales, R., & Pino, J. (2018). Ranas dardo venenosas (*Dendrobatidae*) y su importancia en la bioprospección de moléculas bioactivas en los últimos tiempos: una revisión. *Revista de Investigación Científica (RIC)*, *4* (Especial).

16 Hawksworth, D. L., & Lücking, R. (2017). Fungal diversity revisited: 2.2 to 3.8 million species. *Microbiology Spectrum*, *5*(4).

17 Holgado-Rojas, M. E., Calatayud Hermoza, G., Álvarez Conza, C., & Ccopa Huayta, H. (2019). Diversidad y composición de helechos arbóreos en Winay-Intipunku (SHMP). *Revista Q'euña*, *10*(1), 45-52. Sociedad Botánica del Cusco.

18 Ibáñez Olivera, L. M., & Iannacone Olivers, J. (2011). Ecología y estado de conservación del cóndor de la selva. *Biotempo*, *11*.

19 Larivière, S. (1999). *Lontra longicaudis. Mammalian Species, 609*. American Society of Mammalogists.

20 Lovejoy, T. E., & Nobre, C. (2018). Amazon tipping point. *Science Advances*, *4*(2).

21 Sancho, D., Álvarez Gil, M. J., & Fernández Sánchez, L. R. (2015). Insectos y alimentación. Larvas de *Rhynchophorus palmarum L.*, un alimento de los pobladores de la Amazonía ecuatoriana. *Entomotropica*, *30*(14), 135-149.

22 Santana, O. D. G., *et al.* (2025). Tamandúa: El arte de comer hormigas. *Therya Ixmana*, *4*(1).

23 Serrano, L., & Suárez, Y. (2019). *Características generales e inmunológicas de Aotus sp. y su importancia como modelo animal no humano* [Tesis de grado, Universidad Colegio Mayor de Cundinamarca].

24 Tejedor Garavito, N., Álvarez, E., Arango Caro, S., Cuesta, F., & Kattan, G. (2012). Evaluación del estado de conservación de los bosques montanos en los Andes tropicales. *Ecosistemas*, *21*(1-2), 148-166.

25 Vera, M. F. da S., & Martin, A. R. (2018). Amazon river dolphin: *Inia geoffrensis.* En B. Würsig, J. G. M. Thewissen & K. M. Kovacs (Eds.), *Encyclopedia of marine mammals*. Elsevier.

26 Villa, L., & Finer, M. (2019). *Identificando tala ilegal en la Amazonía peruana.* MAAP, 99. https://maaproject.org/2019/maap99-tala-ilegal/

27 Visalberghi, E. (1990). Tool use in *Cebus*. *Folia Primatologica*, *54*(3-4).

28 Yu, D. W., & Pierce, N. E. (1998). A castration parasite of an ant-plant mutualism. *Proceedings of the Royal Society of London. Series B: Biological Sciences*, *265*(1403), 375-382. https://doi.org/10.1098/rspb.1998.0305

Online Resources

1 Actualidad Ambiental: https://www.actualidadambiental.pe/

2 Aguas Amazónicas: https://aguasamazonicas.org

3 Amazon AID: https://amazonaid.org/los-insectos/

4 Anfibia Web: https://amphibiaweb.org/

5 Animalia: https://animalia.bio/#google_vignette

6 Bird Life: https://www.birdlife.org/

7 Birds of the World (Cornell Lab): https://birdsoftheworld.org

8 Instituto de Investigaciones de la Amazonía Peruana (IIAP): http://www.iiap.org.pe

9 Panel Científico por la Amazonía: https://www.laamazoniaquequeremos.org

10 Proyecto Guacamayo de Tambopata: https://rainforestexpeditions.com/es/proyecto-guacamayo-tambopata/

11 Red Amazónica de Información Socioambiental Georreferenciada (Raisg): https://www.raisg.org / https://www.amazoniasocioambiental.org/es/

12 Reptile Database: http://www.reptile-database.org/

13 ResearchGate: https://www.researchgate.net

14 *Revista Ecosistemas:* https://www.revistaecosistemas.net

15 Royal society: https://royalsociety.org/journals/

16 *ScienceDirect*: https://www.sciencedirect.com

17 Scientific Electronic Library Online (SciELO): http://www.scielo.org.co

18 Servicio Nacional Forestal y de Fauna Silvestre (Serfor): https://www.serfor.gob.pe

19 The Nature Conservancy. (Conservation Gateway): https://www.conservationgateway.org

20 UICN Red List: https://www.iucnredlist.org

21 Wild Life Conservation Society: https://www.wcs.org/

22 WWF: https://wwf.panda.org/